BLOOD BOUGHT

Discovering the truth of our
REDEMPTION

DAVID RAVENHILL

Scripture references taken from various translations.

ISBN 978-0-9767316-2-7

First Printing 2010
Second Printing 2011

Printed in the United States of America

Cover photo by Jim Vallee

Book design by Lorinda Gray/The Ragamuffin Acre
www.ragamuffinphotography.com

THIS BOOK IS DEDICATED TO THE
GLORY OF GOD.

HE ALONE, DESERVES
THE PRAISE AND MAY THE
LAMB THAT WAS SLAIN
RECEIVE THE REWARD
OF HIS SUFFERING.

ENDORSEMENTS

IN HIS LATEST BOOK, *Blood Bought*, David Ravenhill unlocks the secret to man's redemption: the cross. Using poignant illustrations and irrefutable logic, Ravenhill masterfully and systematically lays a biblical foundation for true salvation. In a day when many seem to be deceived, David stands forth and tells the truth. We have been purchased at a frightening cost: the blood of God's very own Son. It is only by embracing the cross of Jesus Christ that we will share His eternal reign.

Steve Gallagher.
Founder, Pure Life Ministry,
Dry Ridge, Kentucky

IN THESE DAYS of superficial spiritual fads and sound-bite Christianity, we need David Ravenhill's voice more than ever. *Blood Bought* gets us back on track, pointing us to the heart of the matter, to the truths that have endured through the generations, to the glorious price that was paid for our redemption. Read this book and be cleansed and empowered afresh!

Dr. Michael L. Brown
President, FIRE School of Ministry,
Concord, North Carolina

WITH JUST A SIMPLE GLANCE at the daily news, we can see that the whole earth is full of shakings, both economically and ecologically. We have seen the horrors of human tragedies depicted on television screens. Truly, everything that can be shaken is being shaken. In some instances, we've seen the exasperation and unnecessary loss of life due to faulty foundations and infrastructures. Sadly, I have personally witnessed this far too often after major natural disasters, even most recently in Haiti.

Conversely, Scripture gives us clear examples of the necessity, both spiritually and practically, to build on a deep and solid foundation, a sure and firm foundation that is unshakable. Yet, it seems that even in the church we have been willing to compromise and cut corners, thus causing many to be shipwrecked. David Ravenhill, in his book Blood Bought, aptly challenges us when he says, "If we fail to understand the full message of the cross, our very foundation is questionable and our faith is faulty at best."

Blood Bought reminds us of the futility of building by any other means than on the foundation of the cross of Christ. I remember learning from David's father, the late Leonard Ravenhill, that many want to experience the power of Pentecost in the upper room, yet think they can do so without going to the cross. It seems there continues to be a "de-Christianizing" and "de-crossing" of the church, thus professing a form of godliness but denying the source of its power. We have propped up the institution without the foundation by which we are endued, thus rendering us powerless to see an authentic transforming revival. It is alarming to see so many professing Christians who do not understand the centrality of their faith, the high cost of Calvary, so great a salvation through Christ at the cross, that provides our redemption.

I would highly recommend setting aside time in a quiet place to read through this book. Let the Holy Spirit give you a fresh revelation of the work of the cross, and rediscover the lost truth of your redemption.

Doug Stringer
Founder/President
Somebody Cares America/International
Turning Point Ministries International
Houston, Texas

ACKNOWLEDGMENTS

IN HIGH SCHOOL, I successfully failed English. I consider myself grammatically challenged, and even to this day, I can't make a decision as to where a sentence should begin or end, let alone know where to place all the commas, semicolons, etc. Thankfully, God gave me Nancy, my wonderful and gifted wife, whose eagle-eye can spot a grammatical mistake a mile away. I would also like to thank Ann Woodruff for helping with the proofreading.

Even though this is my sixth book in print, I still stand back in amazement at what the Lord has done. I have absolutely no ground on which to boast. God, and God alone, deserves the glory for all He has done in and through me.

The writing of this book could never have happened without drawing from the anointed works of great men like Charles Spurgeon, G. Campbell Morgan, John R. Stott, and A. W. Tozer, just to name a few. I was fortunate to have inherited my father's library of several thousand books. This allows me access to many of the writings of these old-time saints. I have sought to weave their insights, along with my own, throughout the following pages.

This is by no means a complete and exhaustive study on the theme of redemption. My prayer is that God would use it to help rally and challenge a new generation of believers to give themselves totally and unreservedly to the one who paid the supreme price, not only for their sin but also for their lives.

TABLE OF CONTENTS

INTRODUCTION

GOD, in His infinite grace, has allowed me to travel extensively throughout the United States and around the world. Over the past forty-five years of ministry, I have endeavored to share the message of the cross wherever I have been privileged to minister. I have been greatly surprised by the response of people to this very vital and simple message. Many will say, "I have never heard the cross preached in such a way before" or "This is the first time I've ever heard such a message." What surprises me the most is why? The cross is the very core, foundation, crux, and center of the Christian faith. If we fail to understand the full message of the cross, our very foundation is questionable and our faith is faulty at best.

My understanding of the cross came over a period of several weeks while working with David Wilkerson's Teen Challenge program in New York City in 1964. My wife, Nancy, and I had recently graduated from Bible college in Minneapolis. The college we attended had a strong emphasis on missions. Both my wife and I planned to head toward the mission field as soon as we had clear direction as to exactly where the Lord would have us labor. One afternoon, while working at Teen Challenge, I found myself asking the question, "Why is the world still unevangelized?" Two thousand years ago, Jesus Christ shed His blood in that great atoning work of Calvary. Two thousand years had passed since Jesus gave His disciples the Great Commission to go into all the world and preach the gospel. Two thousand years had also passed since the outpouring of the Spirit on the

Day of Pentecost when the Church was empowered by the Spirit to fulfill this great purpose of God. Why then had we failed? What was wrong? There had certainly been no failure from God's side. He remains steadfast in His purpose that "none should perish" (2 Pet. 3:9). As I pondered upon these things, the Lord seemed to impress on me that the fault lay with us. The fault in this case was a failure on our part to preach and teach the message of the cross. This failure has had catastrophic results both in the Church and in the world at large. The Church will never regain her true calling until we correct this serious doctrinal error.

One can never fully grasp all there is to know about the atoning work of Christ. I believe even in eternity we will still stand in awe of all that Christ accomplished on the cross. Only the other day I was reading This Was His Faith, a collection of letters written by G. Campbell Morgan, in which he writes:

> To come to the great subject, which you say, you still find confusing; the fact that Christ died to save. It is an old question, the central problem and mystery of our faith. I want at once to add, as a word of personal testimony, that I think I have read all the great works on the Atonement, and from every one of them I have derived some help; but they always leave me with the feeling that in the fact of the death of Christ there is something more than has been, and I think than ever can be, interpreted.[1]

I wholeheartedly agree with G. Campbell Morgan that the scope of the cross is far beyond man's ability to fully interpret. In the following pages, we want to explore the great truth of our redemption. In 1962, Thomas Watson wrote the following: "The doctrine of redemption by Jesus Christ is a glorious doctrine; it is the marrow and quintessence of the gospel…Great was the work of creation, but greater the work of redemption; it cost more to redeem us than to make us; in the one there was but the speaking of a word, in the other the shedding of blood."[2]

My prayer is that you, the reader, will come into a greater understanding of the height, breadth, and depth of Christ's great and glorious redemptive work.

[1] G. Campbell Morgan, *This Was His Faith* (London: Pickering & Inglis Ltd., 1952), 188.
[2] Thomas Watson, *A Body of Divinity* (Carlisle, PA: Banner of Truth Trust. 1992), 209.

CHAPTER ONE

Contending
for the Faith

*Beloved, while I was making every effort to write
to you about our common salvation, I felt the
necessity to write to you appealing that you
contend earnestly or the faith which was once for
all delivered to the saints. For certain persons have
crept in unnoticed, those who were long beforehand
marked out for this condemnation, ungodly persons
who turn the grace of our God into licentiousness
and deny our only Master and Lord, Jesus Christ.*

JUDE 3-4

Enter any jewelry store and you will find crosses for sale. Prices range from just a few dollars to thousands. They come in every material known to man, from wood to plastic or from jade to gold, from plain to diamond studded, from small to large. Whatever strikes your fancy, there is a cross available. Yes, the cross is now an ornament to display with pride. It is something that hopefully will enhance your overall appearance and make you "look good."

Two thousand years ago, the cross was to be feared, dreaded, shunned, and avoided at all costs. The cross conveyed only one message: death. How times have changed! Today the cross is simply viewed as a free pass that will guarantee you access through the pearly gates when the time comes. Some consider it a lucky charm that offers some form of protection when worn around the neck. Sadly, the church has failed to proclaim the true message of the cross.

As A. W. Tozer writes in the following excerpt, there is a vast difference between the old cross and the new.

The Old Cross and the New

"UNANNOUNCED AND MOSTLY UNDETECTED, there has come in modern times a new cross into popular evangelical circles. It is like the old cross but different: the likenesses are superficial; the differences, fundamental. From this new cross has sprung a new philosophy of the Christian life, and from that new philosophy has come a new evangelical technique—a new type of meeting and a new kind of preaching. This new evangelism employs the same language as the old, but its content is not the same and its emphasis not as before.

The old cross would have no [1]truck with the world. For Adam's proud flesh it meant the end of the journey. It carried into effect the sentence imposed by the law of Sinai. The new cross is not opposed to the human race; rather, it is a friendly pal and, if understood aright, it is the source of oceans of good clean fun and innocent enjoyment. It lets Adam live without interference. His life motivation is unchanged; he still lives for his own pleasure, only now he takes delight in singing choruses and watching religious movies instead of singing bawdy songs and drinking hard liquor. The accent is still on enjoyment, though the fun is now on a higher plane morally if not intellectually.

The new cross encourages a new and entirely different evangelistic approach. The evangelist does not demand abnegation of the old life before a new life can be received. He preaches not contrasts but similarities. He seeks to key into public interest by showing that Christianity makes no unpleasant demands; rather, it offers the same thing the world does, only on a higher level. Whatever the sin-mad world happens to be clamoring after at the moment is cleverly shown to be the very thing the gospel offers, only the religious product is better.

The new cross does not slay the sinner, it redirects him. It gears him into a cleaner and jollier

1 exchange or barter

way of living exchange or barter and saves his self-respect. To the self-assertive it says, "Come and assert yourself for Christ."

To the egotist it says, "Come and do your boasting in the Lord." To the thrill seeker it says, "Come and enjoy the thrill of Christian fellowship." The Christian message is slanted in the direction of the current vogue in order to make it acceptable to the public.

The philosophy in back of this kind of thing may be sincere, but its sincerity does not save it from being false. It is false because it is blind. It misses completely the whole meaning of the cross.

The old cross is a symbol of death. It stands for the abrupt, violent end of a human being. The man in Roman times who took up his cross and started down the road had already said good-bye to his friends. He was not coming back. He was going out to have it ended. The cross made no compromise, modified nothing, spared nothing; it slew all of the man, completely and for good. It did not try to keep on good terms with its victim. It struck cruel and hard, and when it had finished its work, the man was no more.

The race of Adam is under death sentence. There is no commutation and no escape. God cannot approve any of the fruits of sin, however innocent they may appear or beautiful to the eyes of men. God salvages the individual by liquidating him and then raising him again to newness of life. That evangelism which draws friendly parallels between the ways of God and the ways of men is false to the Bible and cruel to the souls of its hearers. The faith of Christ does not parallel the world, it intersects it. In coming to Christ we do not bring our old life up onto a higher plane; we leave it at the cross. The grain of wheat must fall into the ground and die.

We who preach the gospel must not think of ourselves as public relations agents sent to establish good will between Christ and the world. We must not imagine ourselves commissioned to make Christ acceptable to big business, the press, the world of sports, or modern education. We are not diplomats but prophets, and our message is not a compromise but an ultimatum.

God offers life, but not an improved old life. The life He offers is life out of death. It stands always on the far side of the cross. Whoever would possess it must pass under the rod. He must repudiate himself and concur in God's just sentence against him.

What does this mean to the individual, the condemned man who would find life in Christ Jesus? How can this theology be translated into life? Simply, he must repent and believe. He must forsake his sins and then go on to forsake himself. Let him cover nothing, defend nothing, excuse nothing. Let him not seek to make terms with God, but let him bow his head before the stroke of God's stern displeasure and acknowledge himself worthy to die. Having done this let him gaze with simple trust upon the risen Savior, and from Him will come life and rebirth and cleansing and power. The cross that ended the earthly life of Jesus now puts an end to the sinner; and the power that raised Christ from the dead now raises him to a new life along with Christ.

To any who may object to this or count it merely a narrow and private view of truth, let me say God has set His hallmark of approval upon this message from Paul's day to the present. Whether stated in these exact words or not, this has been the content of all preaching that has brought life and power to the world through the centuries. The mystics, the reformers, the revivalists have put their emphasis here, and signs and wonders and mighty operations of the Holy Ghost gave witness to God's approval. Dare we, the heirs of such a legacy of power, tamper with the truth? Dare we with our stubby pencils erase the lines of the blueprint or alter the pattern shown us in the Mount? May God forbid. Let us preach the old cross and we will know the old power.

—A. W. Tozer, *Man, the Dwelling Place of God*, 1966.
Used by permission of the Alliance Witness [3]

There is little doubt in my mind that the writers of the New Testament would cringe in horror if they were to attend the average church meeting today. The message of the cross has undergone major modification over the centuries. We have gradually changed its message from God's purpose to man's pleasure. Instead of the cross being a means of death, it has become a means of desire.

Allow me to explain. In Jude's epistle, Jude sets off to write about "our common salvation" but then changes his mind and writes, "I felt the necessity to write to you appealing that you contend earnestly for the faith which was once delivered to the saints." He then seeks to expose those who "turn the grace of God into licentiousness and deny the only Master and Lord, Jesus Christ." Jude is deeply distressed by those within the church who were teaching a message of "greasy grace" (the belief that we can go on sinning because we remain under God's protective grace). He is also deeply troubled by those who refuse to acknowledge Christ as Master and Lord. Lordship has been taught as an optional extra. You can accept Christ as Savior, and if you care to go the second mile, as Lord and Master. Accepting Christ as Savior is not an option if you intend to make it to heaven, but Lordship comes with certain "restrictions" that tend to place limitations on what one can do with one's life. As Americans, we are raised on the belief that this is the "home of the brave and the land of the free." Who then wants to have his or her freedoms restricted?

Today we want a "cross" that will work for us, not against us. In other words, we want to have our own way, and the old cross doesn't allow that. Before closing this chapter, I want to look at the story Jesus told of the two men who built similar houses. One, you recall, was built on the sand; the other built his house on the rock. Both houses were fine until the winds, rain, and floods came. It was only then that their differences became apparent. One was swept away and destroyed while the other remained steadfast and immovable. According to Webster's Dictionary, the word sand is defined as: "loose granular material resulting from the disintegration of rock."[4] In other words, sand is small pieces of rock that were once a part of the whole rock. There is a grave danger in building our faith on "fragments" of God's Word, avoiding those areas that fail to meet with our best interests.

Well, I'm already getting ahead of myself, so let's pause for awhile and take a journey back in time.

[3] A. W. Tozer, Man, *The Dwelling Place Of God*. (Camp Hill, PA: Christian Publications, Inc. 1966)

[4] *Webster's New Collegiate Dictionary*. (Springfield, MA: G & C Merriam, 1959), 748.

Contending for the Faith

CHAPTER TWO

Back to the Beginning

And as Moses lifted up the serpent in the wilderness,
even so must the Son of Man be lifted up;
that whoever believes may have eternal life.

JOHN 3:14-15

Over the centuries, the Church has viewed the cross as her own. That is to say we have considered the cross primarily given for our benefit. This in turn has resulted in a greatly distorted view of the cross, placing man at the center rather than God.

The cross was given by God as a medicine for man's sickness. It was to bring restoration to all man's ills and restore him to God's initial purpose and plan.

Imagine waking up in the morning to find that every muscle in your body feels like it has been run over by a Mack truck. Added to that, you can barely breathe and have a constant cough and blinding headache. You immediately head to your physician seeking help. After thoroughly checking you over, he prescribes several medications, advising you to rest, drink plenty of fluids, and take the entire recommended dose of prescribed pills. Returning home, you follow your physician's orders to the letter. A week goes by and you still have the same symptoms. Another week and you still feel the same as the first day. You decide to make another appointment to see your physician, seeking an explanation as to why you're still feeling the same. You reason in your mind that if these pills really worked, you would be back to normal by now. Obviously something is wrong. Either the physician has misdiagnosed your condition, or there is something wrong with the medication. How do you know all this? Simply because you still have the same symptoms. Medicine, if working correctly, should bring about full restoration.

The cross, as stated, is God's medicine for man's diseased soul. Allow me to expound on this point, as it forms the foundation of all that this book is predicated on.

Jesus, speaking of His death, made the following statement: "As Moses lifted up the serpent in the wilderness, even so must the Son of Man be lifted up" (John 3:14). The Jews were immediately reminded of their time in the wilderness when, because of their sin and rebellion, God permitted serpents to come into the camp, destroying thousands of Israelites. Only when Moses cried out to God did God respond by telling Moses to form a brazen serpent and place it on a pole, so that whoever looked upon it would live.

One can imagine the following scenario: An Israelite father walks into his tent, complaining to his family about Moses's leadership. He is angry and venting his feelings on all who will listen. Suddenly a serpent slithers under the corner of the tent and strikes the man. Immediately upon being struck, he senses his strength beginning to ebb away. Soon he finds himself too weak to stand and collapses on the tent floor. His family stands there terrified as they watch him begin to go into convulsions, his body shaking like a leaf in the wind. They cry out for help. Soon a neighbor responds, telling them that there is a cure. God instructed Moses to make a brazen serpent, telling them that whoever looked upon it would be healed. The family quickly responds by dragging their almost-dead father out of the tent and lifting his face toward the brazen serpent. Almost instantly they begin to see a change. His face quickly begins to regain its color. His body stops convulsing. His strength steadily but surely returns, and within a short period of time, he is fully restored back to life.

Prior to his rebellion against the leadership, he was his former self. His mind was clear, his body functioning normally, and he was able to go about his daily routine.

The lesson here is obvious; the brazen serpent restored every transgressor back to his or her former condition. This is the message Jesus sought to convey when He likened His death to that of being raised up like the brazen serpent.

In the beginning when man sinned in the Garden, the serpent injected his deadly venom into our first parents, causing them to lose their original pure and innocent position and calling.

Allow me to further illustrate this by taking you around the neighborhood, hunting for treasure at the local garage sales. As you drive by one of the houses, you notice an old dresser for sale. You momentarily forget about looking for some treasure, remembering that your daughter could use a dresser in her room. After haggling over the price, you load the dresser into your pickup, along with other items you have purchased. Several weeks later, a friend drops by for a visit and notices the dresser. She advises you that what you considered just another dresser is in fact a genuine antique worth thousands if properly restored. After doing your own research, you too are convinced that what she told you is right. You decide to take the dresser to a certified restorer of antiques. The craftsman examines the piece and informs you that your dresser is in fact extremely rare and worth considerably more than you had originally been told. He then informs you of the cost of restoration, letting you know that in its present condition it has little value.

He invites you into his showroom and proceeds to show you a similar dresser that has been restored. You gaze in wonderment at the beauty and craftsmanship and the potential of how your piece of junk is capable of being restored and gladly agree to the restoration process.

Several weeks go by as you anticipate seeing your dresser again in its restored condition. Imagine then your utter disappointment and anger when upon returning to collect your dresser you find it freshly painted in white with red acrylic knobs. The value of the dresser has diminished by thousands of dollars. Only when restored to its original condition has it any real value.

This is not unlike the modern method of preaching the cross. Instead of informing man of God's original intent, we tend rather to spray paint man according to what we think looks good. It is a cheap imitation, at best, of what God had in mind when He first created him. Hopefully by now you are beginning to see that it is only as we are restored to God's original purpose that we can say we have been born again.

This is what the cross is all about—restoration. If medicine fails to restore us to health, we rightly complain or switch physicians, and yet when it comes to the greatest medicine of all, the cross, we're content with our white paint and red acrylic knobs.

30

CHAPTER THREE

The Garden, Man's Original Home

Then the Lord took the man and put him into the garden of Eden to cultivate it and keep it.

GENESIS 2:8, 15

Several years ago, my wife and I had the honor of being invited to Rome, Italy, to minister. While in Rome, we had the opportunity to visit the Vatican and view one of the world's greatest works of art, the ceiling of the Sistine Chapel. This incredible fresco by Michelangelo had just been painstakingly restored by a process that had taken many years to complete. Prior to the restoration, art historians had declared Michelangelo to be one of the greatest sculptors of all time but said that he was an artist who "painted with a dark palette." Following its completion in 1509, this incredible masterpiece had over the past five hundred years suffered the devastating effects of carbon soot that had ascended from the numerous candles used to light this magnificent chapel. The November issue of Life magazine carried this headline on its cover: "First pictures of Michelangelo's Sistine Chapel as it hasn't been seen in five hundred years—A CLEAR VIEW OF HEAVEN." The restoration, finally completed, revealed for the first time in centuries the blaze of brilliant and vivid colors. The art world was stunned and embarrassed as they beheld this once-drab fresco now restored to its former glory.

For too long, the Church has grown to accept a drab form of Christianity due largely to the buildup of compromise around the teaching of the cross. My hope and prayer is that as we systematically expose the "soot," we will see once again God's great and glorious purpose behind the cross.

As I have stated in the last chapter, any work of restoration requires the restorer to know what the item looked like originally. Since the cross is God's means of restoring man, it is essential that we understand God's plan and purpose for man from the beginning.

Allow me to begin by turning our attention to several verses in John's First Epistle, beginning 2:12–14. In these three verses of Scripture, John addresses children, young men, and fathers. John is not addressing three age groups but rather three levels of spiritual maturity. Just as we progress physically from children to youth, then on to adulthood, so likewise in the spiritual realm. Nobody is born fully developed physically, emotionally, or mentally. John begins by telling the children that their sins are forgiven. Just as a baby in the natural has no past, so it is likewise in the spiritual realm. If a newborn could articulate why it's crying, you would never hear it say, "I'm bothered by all the sins I've committed over the years." The fact is, a baby has no past to be troubled over. The newborn Christian, the moment he repents of sin and by faith takes hold of God's redeeming grace, is forgiven of his past. John then goes on to say that children know their fathers. One of the first relationships a child has is with his father. The first cry of the newborn believer is Abba or daddy/father.

John then goes on to address the young men, saying, "You are strong and the Word of God abides in you and you have overcome the evil one." As a child matures into a young man, he is faced with having to make his own decisions and must learn to stand on his own two feet. He is no longer carried, coddled, and cared for by his parents. The Christian likewise has to learn to stand against all the wiles of the evil one. His only means of doing so is to know who he is in Christ. Here is where the importance of God's Word comes in. As he nourishes his soul on the milk of God's Word, he becomes strong and able to combat all the attacks of the enemy.

Finally John turns his attention to the fathers. Now let me pause here and say that for many years I was totally disappointed by how John describes these mature believers. Twice he repeats, "Because you know Him that is from the beginning." Is that the best he can come up with? Isn't he repeating what he has already said to the children, "You know the Father"? If I were writing about the third stage of spiritual maturity, I would have said something awesome such as, "I write to you fathers because you have memorized the entire Pentateuch. Not only that, but you understand the books of Daniel and Revelation perfectly." Or perhaps I would remind them of the numerous forty-day fasts they had completed. You get the idea. Something that makes them look worthy of being referred to as fathers.

As I've pondered these verses, I've come to realize that there is a vast difference between the way a child knows his father and "knowing Him that is from the beginning." A child knows his father from a very self-centered position. His father exists largely to feed, clothe, comfort, care, and protect him. Most children never think of the needs of their father, or for that matter, ever worry over what their father may be doing. Now don't take this in a wrong way—that's quite normal for every child both naturally as well as spiritually. The key to John's brief description of the fathers lies in this word "beginning." Perhaps we could best describe the three levels this way:

Children—Regeneration
Young Men—Maturation
Fathers—Consummation/Culmination

One of John's favorite expressions is the use of the word "beginning." He opens his Gospel with "In the beginning…" He begins his Epistle with, "What was from the beginning…"

In his Revelation, he refers to Jesus as "the beginning and the end." John uses this word beginning more that all the other writers of the Bible. Fathers understand God, not simply as father the way a child would but with the greater understanding of all that God is and has purposed. Fathers see the big picture. They comprehend their relationship to God's eternal plan and purpose as it pertains to the beginning of things.

Allow me to elaborate on this if you will. Many of the old expositors would refer to what they called the "Law of first mention" or the "Law of beginnings." They stressed the importance of seeing things from God's perspective. Let me illustrate what I mean. You recall how the Scribes and Pharisees were constantly attempting to trap Jesus by asking difficult questions. On this occasion, they are questioning Him about marriage and in particular about divorce. There were two popular schools of thought at the time. One was extremely liberal, the other very conservative. Jesus was not about to identify with either one but rather sought to draw their attention back to God's original purpose concerning marriage and so replied, "In the beginning it was not so."

It is only when we go back to the beginning that we have a clear perspective of God's original plan and purpose for man. We do, after all, live in the midst of a "crooked and perverse generation."

Since none of us were alive from the beginning, we have never seen clearly. Instead we see through a glass darkly, so to speak. It's akin to being given someone else's glasses with the hope that they will help you see better, only to discover that everything is blurred and out of focus. This is the world we live in. Everything has been distorted by sin and therefore resembles only a caricature of what it should be like.

Only as we understand God's original intentions for man can we appreciate the full impact of all that the cross was intended to do.

Genesis is called the book of beginnings. In the first three chapters, we are introduced to marriage, sin, judgment, sacrifice, etc. What we want to look at now is what man looked like in God's original order of things. In the 2:15 we read, "Then the Lord God took the man and put him in the Garden of Eden to cultivate it and to keep it."

Three things immediately become obvious when looking at this verse.

1. Submission
2. Location
3. Vocation

Man was totally submitted to God when first formed. God was able to take him without any objection on man's part. Man did not stand defiantly opposing what God wanted to do with him, but rather yielded himself fully in submission to the Lord.

God then placed man in a specific location—namely the Garden of Eden. Man was not left to wonder where he should be or live. God had a specific place in mind for him. Finally, after placing man in the Garden, God revealed his vocation or calling for man. God told Adam that he was to cultivate and keep the garden. Once again, man is not left to figure out what he is supposed to do with his life.

Here we have a brief glimpse of what I believe the cross is all about. God sought, through the cross, to restore man back to His original goal and purpose.

This will become more evident as we look at other Scriptures along these same lines. It is only as we attempt to understand the mind of God for man from the beginning that we can ever fully grasp the meaning of the cross.

CHAPTER FOUR

Understanding the Mind of God

*For by Him all things were created, both in the heavens
and on earth, visible and invisible, whether thrones
or dominions or rulers or authorities—all things
have been created by Him and for Him.*

COLOSSIANS 1:16

Paul's epistle to the Colossians gives us a further key to God's intention for man from the beginning. Notice what Paul writes in 1:16: "For by Him all things were created, both in the heavens and on the earth, visible and invisible, whether thrones or dominions or rulers or authorities—all things were created by Him..." Most believing Christians have little if any problem believing that God created the heavens and the earth. We simply take it for granted or acknowledge it as a fact without even batting an eye. We don't take it personally but rather factually. Paul, however, does not end with, "all things were created by Him" but adds "and *for Him*." This has an immediate bearing on my life and yours. *We* were created *for Him*. That was why God created man—for *Himself*. God never intended for man to wander around doing whatever he pleases whenever he pleases. Man was created for a purpose

We are told in the book of Revelation, "Worthy art Thou, our Lord and our God, to receive glory and honor and power, for Thou didst create all things...." Once again we are told that God alone is the One who created the heavens and earth. The verse goes on to tell us the reason why God created these things: "And because of Thy will they existed and were created." The King James Version states it this way: "And for Your pleasure they were created."

When we look into the mind of God as revealed to us through His Word, we discover that God created man for His will, pleasure, and purpose.

Now let's examine another verse, this time in the writing to the Hebrews. In the 2:10 we read, "For it was fitting for

Him for whom are all things, and through whom are all things...." Allow me to reverse the order of these two phrases in keeping with the other verses. For it was fitting for Him through whom are all things and for whom are all things. Through whom reveals the source; for whom reveals the purpose.

Finally, let's look at this amazing revelation in the letter to the Romans. Most Christians are aware of this verse and can immediately quote it to you when asked: "I beseech you therefore brethren by the mercies of God that you present your bodies a living and holy sacrifice..." (Rom. 12:1). Like a jewel taken from its setting, we have failed to see the real value of this verse. Allow me to go back to the final verse of the previous chapter, for without this setting, we will fail to grasp the full significance of what Paul is saying. In 11:36, we have one of the most amazing verses in the Bible in regard to God and His purposes. I personally believe that this revelation had as great an impact on Paul's life as any other we are told about. This verse is one of both *creation* and *culmination* (or *consummation*) as it reveals the big picture like no other. Read it carefully: "For from Him and through Him and to Him are all things. To Him be the glory forever. Amen." Picture in your mind a triangle. Going down the left side is *from Him*, across the bottom is *through Him*, and then going up the right side is *to Him*.

Everything has it origin from God. He is the Creator of all things. There are numerous references throughout God's Word explaining this simple yet profound truth. God is not just the Creator of all things but also the *Sustainer* of all things. He holds all things together by the word of His power. It is in Him we live and move and have our very being. But that is not all. He is also the *Consummator* of all things: "And to *Him* are all things." What God started, He will finish. He is both *Author* and *Finisher* of all things. *Therefore*, I beseech you, brethren, that you present your body (which is *from Him, through Him*, and therefore *to Him*) as a living sacrifice.

Paul leaves us without excuse. If God created us and sustains us and sees us as His own, then how can we not—given that revelation—give ourselves to Him as an act of worship?

It is only as we go back to an understanding of God's original intent for man that we can proceed with what God had in mind when He sent Christ to die.

Imagine discovering a sixty-five-year-old vintage car in some farmer's dilapidated barn. After making some inquiries, you find the name of the farmer and ask him if he would sell you his car. Having acquired the car, you begin the restoration process. Throughout the long winter months, you painstakingly strip the car back to bare metal. Meanwhile, you have sent the engine to be rebuilt by a local mechanic. Although the car was basically intact when you discovered it, it did lack wheels, headlights, and fenders. Several months pass, and the once-shabby car now sports a beautiful coat of burgundy red paint, while the roof and fenders are painted black.

Once the engine is installed, the only things missing are the wheels, headlights, and fenders. Never having seen an original model of this car, you make the decision that a pair of small halogen headlights would look great and that some ultra-wide mag wheels and fatso tires would give the car the look it needs. Once the wheels and headlights are fitted, the car is almost ready to drive. The only remaining items necessary are the front and rear fenders. Unable to decide what looks good, you settle upon a pair of modern fenders from the local wrecker's yard. After painting them to match the rest of the car, you are finally ready to enjoy your hard work.

The car starts without any trouble, and you set off down the road. Heads turn as you drive by. This has been the reaction you had hoped for. You decide to head for town, where you know there will be more admirers. Sure enough, as you slow to turn a corner, an old man stares almost in disbelief at what he sees. Since there is a parking place close by, you stop to allow the man time to really see all you have accomplished. Immediately he asks you, "What is the make of the car?" You inform him that it is a certain make, model, and year. He points his finger at you and says, "Son, that's not the way I remember them looking." He then proceeds to point out all the modifications you have made that were never part of the original design.

I don't want to labor the point, but this is exactly what we have done with the preaching of the cross. Not realizing God's original design for man, we have set about to restore man without seeing the original plans.

CHAPTER FIVE

Back to the Garden

*And the Lord God planted a garden
toward the east, in Eden; and there
He placed the man whom He had formed.*

GENESIS 2:8

The world is an amazing place. Every continent has its own unique beauty. I have traveled quite extensively and never tire of the vast variety of landscapes that make up this magnificent world of ours. Consider the great mountain ranges, the vast deserts, the long, serpentine rivers, the sprawling prairies, and the dense jungles. Then there are the mighty oceans with thousands of islands, looking like freckles on a kid's face.

But imagine what it must have been like before it was subjected to bondage and ravished by rebellion and sin. What we see now is a mere shadow of what it was when God first created it. Yes, the ground has been cursed and bears little, if any, resemblance to its former glory.

There is little doubt that the crowning achievement of creation, apart from the creation of man, was the Garden of Eden. This garden paradise was not only man's earthly abode but also God's. It was here that God came in the cool of the day to fellowship with Adam and Eve. This was really God's home or house. Yes, we could even say this was the first temple in the Bible. You see that when the Bible says that God planted a garden in Eden. The word used for planted means to drive in tent pegs—at least that is the root meaning. The word garden means a hedged place or fenced place. In other words, God formed an enclosure by driving in tent pegs. This then became man's first home. The only entrance was on the east. All of this corresponds to the tabernacle and the temple. Well over a hundred years ago, Robert Govett explained that in every temple or tabernacle made by man, man could only create a laver. Yet in every temple made by

God, there is always a river. From Eden a river flowed that brought life to the surrounding regions. Here in this fenced place God dwelt and communed with man. It was only after the fall of man that man was banished from God's house and presence and had to leave the garden.

Prior to man's sin, he was given authority to subdue the earth. Are you beginning to see a little glimpse of what God intended? Man, in fellowship with God and living in obedience, was to work from God's temple, under God's authority, and subdue the earth.

What Happened?

The Bible is clear in regard to the fall of man, but pinpointing the fall of the devil presents a greater dilemma. For some unknown reason, we readily accept the fact that the devil and his angels revolted against God and His angels many millennia before creation. Nobody can say for certain. However, we do have some very thought-provoking Scriptures that may give us a glimpse into what transpired.

One would assume that the angels were created along with the rest of creation and not in some prior creation. Angels, we are told, are ministering spirits sent out on behalf of God's children. Following the creation of Adam and Eve, God never warns them about the enemy. One would think that if the devil was on the prowl that God would have said to Adam and Eve, "From any tree of the garden you may eat freely; but from the tree of the knowledge of good and evil you shall not eat, for from the day that you eat from it you shall surely die. Oh! And by the way, watch out for that sneaky snake. He's deadly." But God never does. This is not consistent with the rest of the Scriptures where we are constantly warned about the enemy's devices.

Not only do we have no warning about the devil, but we are also told that everything God made was either good or very good. That certainly can't be said of the devil. I have long held to the belief that the fall of man and the fall of the devil and his angels were virtually simultaneous events. Here is my reasoning.

Following the creation of the tabernacle in the Garden of Eden, God assigned Lucifer as the guardian angel. "You were in Eden, the Garden of God, every precious stone was thy covering...You were the anointed cherub who guards" (Ezek. 28:11, 14). To the best of my knowledge, heaven is never described as the Garden of Eden.

Lucifer would have seen the daily interaction that the Lord had with man in the Garden. Every day he would see God share His heart with Adam and Eve in fellowship and deep, loving affection. As the days turned into weeks and the weeks turned into years, something began to grow within him. He became jealous of the deepening relationship that he saw growing between God and man and longed to have that same worship directed toward himself. He said to himself, "I will be like the Most High." Realizing that God had given man the capacity of free will, he concocted a subtle yet deadly plan to lure Adam and Eve away from God and deceive them into the belief that they could be like God. All he had to do was convince them that what God said was not really true. He cast doubt on God's Word and any possibility of punishment.

Being the "covering cherub," he had daily access to Adam and Eve. They had come to trust him due to his "wisdom and incredible beauty" (Ezek. 28:11). His cunningly devised plan in place, he waited for the perfect moment to strike. Eve, being weaker than Adam, was first offered his deadly bait. First she resisted by telling the devil that they were not to take or touch the fruit of the tree. The devil was prepared. "You surely shall not die! For God knows that in the day you eat from it your eyes will be opened, and you will be like God, knowing good and evil."

Tragically, Eve, followed by Adam, took from the fruit and ate. How long they had been in the Garden at this stage we do not know. What we do know is that God said, "For in the day that you eat from it, you shall surely die." Since a day with the Lord is a thousand years, we know that Adam never reached that age but died at the age of 930 years—a little short of one day.

Following their sin of disobedience, they immediately recognized that they lost their "glory" and were now naked. They desperately tried to cover themselves by their own works and then sought to hide from their daily appointment with God. They heard Him calling but retreated deeper and deeper into the Garden, aware for the first time that they stood guilty and defiled before their God and creator.

Adam sought to blame Eve for everything. Eve immediately placed all the blame on the serpent. Here is where we find some interesting and vital information. God told the serpent that because of his action, he is cursed. Now we have no statement that he was cursed prior to this. God goes on to say, "On your belly you shall go," meaning he was not on his belly prior to this time. He was then told, "Dust shall you eat," meaning before this time he was not eating dust. Now we come to the most interesting statement of all: "And I will put enmity between you and the woman, and between your seed and her seed; He shall bruise you on the head and you shall bruise him on the heel." Here we are clearly told that at the time of Eve's disobedience, there was not enmity between the serpent and Adam and Eve. Undoubtedly, there was a major fall at this time, not only of Adam and Eve but also of the serpent. If there was no enmity, then the serpent, prior to this, was not their enemy and posed no threat. Certainly God never warned them about the serpent, which any responsible father would be inclined to do. He only warned them about not eating of the fruit of the tree.

While the above scenario may or may not be true, we do know that the devil succeeded in deceiving man into the belief that he was better off making his own plans and serving his own interests rather than in serving and obeying the Lord God.

This was the origin of sin—disobedience. Paul tells us, "For as through the one man's disobedience the many were made sinners" (Rom. 5:19). Ever since that time, mankind has been pursuing his own way and placing his own interests ahead of God's.

Although God created man with the ability to choose, He was not caught off guard by man's disobedience. God already had a plan in place to bruise the serpent's head and to restore man for His glory and purpose.

Back to the Garden

CHAPTER SIX

What is Sin?

*All of us like sheep have gone astray, each of us
has turned to his own way; but the Lord has
caused the iniquity of us all to fall on Him.*
ISAIAH 53:6

*For all have sinned and
fall short of the glory of God.*
ROMANS 3:23

By far the most common New Testament word for sin is the Greek word *Hamartia*. It occurs some sixty times in Paul's letters alone. In classical Greek, it carried the meaning of "failure" or "to miss the mark," as when an arrow missed the target. It could also describe a person who missed the road he was to travel on.

Listen to what William Barclay has to say about sin.

One of the best ways of discovering the real meaning of any word is to examine the company it keeps. A word's meaning, and its inward flavor, will be best found by examining the words in whose company it is usually found.

Let us, then, examine the words with which Hamartia is found in the New Testament:

(i) Hamartia is connected with blasphemia (Matthew 12:31). The basic meaning of blasphemia is insult. Sin is then an insult to God. It insults God by flouting his commandments, by putting self in the place He ought to occupy, and above all by grieving His love.

(ii) Hamartia is connected with apatē. Apatē is "deceit." Sin is always a deceitful thing, in that it promises to do that which it cannot do. Sin is always a lie. Any man who sins, who does the forbidden thing or who takes the forbidden thing, does so because he thinks that he will be happier for doing or taking the thing.

(iii) Hamartia is equated with anomia (1 John 3:4). Anomia is "lawlessness." Sin is that which every now and then makes a man desire to kick over the traces, to have done with restraints and controls, to do exactly as he likes. Anomia is the spirit which makes a man desire to erect his own wishes above his duty to man and his obedience to God. Anomia springs basically from the desire to install self and not God at the center of life.

(iv) Hamartia is connected to prosopolepsia (James 2:9). Prosopolepsia is 'respect of person'. Now respect of persons is the result of applying man's standards instead of God's standards to the world, and to life, and to people in general.[5]

Barclay lists several other words used in connection to sin, but it becomes evident from this list that sin stands in total defiance against God and His purposes. The very essence of sin is that of serving self. It is little wonder, then, that Jesus repeatedly challenged His followers to die to self. We don't see Jesus coming up with a list of sins that had to be forsaken in order to qualify as a disciple. Instead He tackles the very root of man's rebellion by challenging him to die. Dead men have no rights. Dead men don't insist on going their own way. Dead men don't have any interests of their own.

Isaiah summarizes man's condition this way: "All we like sheep have gone astray, we have turned every man to his own way." Regardless of whether he be rich or poor, educated or uneducated, civilized or uncivilized, male or female, every person outside of Christ is living for his own selfish gratification. He has purposely set his heart on doing his own thing.

Since God created man for His pleasure and purpose, these two goals can never be reconciled. One has to die. It is either my way or God's way, but not both.

Why is dying to self so hard? From the moment of birth, self occupies the throne of our life. Consider the following. At the moment of birth, we are greeted with joy and excitement. The doctor, nurse, or midwife announces a beautiful baby has been born. Within hours, family members and friends join in celebrating your birth. Soon you are being passed around and admired. Everyone wants to hold, kiss, cuddle, and rock you. You immediately sense your importance. You are loved, and rightly so. It feels good to be so welcomed into the world.

After your first feeding, you doze off in your mother's arms. A noise wakens you. You stare but can't see a thing. Everything around you is in darkness. Gone are the fans and feelings. You are all alone. Your first response is to let out a cry, first one and then another. Soon the door opens, on goes the light, and before you know it, you are back in your mother's arms again. Your little mind remembers the process. A cry brings an immediate response. And so begins the process of getting "our own way." As we develop, we learn to perfect the art of selfishness. Those with siblings soon learn to become little "Jacobs," knowing how to con their older brother out of his birthright. Soon the world begins to revolve around us. From the schoolyard where we play, "I'm the king of the castle" to the choices we make in life, all tend to foster our selfish independence.

Death is something we all have to eventually face—not only physical death that we do our very best to postpone, but when it comes to the Christian life, volitional death or death to self, to our own way. Just like physical death, we will do anything and everything to avoid it. After all, this is the only life we have ever known. As Americans, we even celebrate our independence every Fourth of July. We have a "bill of rights" to protect our interests. The British proudly sing one of their favorite anthems, "Rule Britannia," in which one lines state, "Britain never, never, never, shall be slaves." The idea of losing our independence is foreign to everything we hold dear. Just as we would fight for our lives in the natural, so likewise we fight for our lives spiritually.

This is where the problem begins. How do I reconcile my rights with the will and purpose of God?

---

[5] William Barclay, *New Testament Words* (London: SCM Press, 1973), 118.

CHAPTER SEVEN

The Kingdom of God

Pilate therefore said to Him, "So you are a king?"
Jesus answered, "You say correctly that I am a king.
For this I have been born, and for this
I have come into the world...

JOHN 18:37

M el Gibson's film *The Passion*, was a box office hit, not to mention a financial bonanza. I seldom meet a Christian who has not watched it and been deeply stirred by it. One would have to be made of stone to not be moved by the intense suffering Jesus endured both prior to and on the cross. While the director did his best to portray all the gory details from the scourging of the whip, the driving in of the nails, to the jeering of the crowds, he failed to portray another aspect of Christ's suffering. Isaiah the prophet tells us, "His appearance was marred more than any man." This was due to them plucking out the hairs of His beard, leaving His face virtually unrecognizable.

No man has ever suffered the way Jesus suffered. "He bore our grief and carried our sorrows…He was smitten by God and afflicted. He was pierced through for our transgressions and crushed for our iniquities; the chastening for our well being fell upon Him and by His scourging we are healed" (Isa. 53:4–5).

But there was more, for according to most authorities, Jesus would have been stark naked on the cross and had to suffer the utter humiliation of being looked upon by the eyes of all.

When asked the simple question, "Why was Jesus crucified?" Most Christians reply by quoting John 3:16: "For God so loved the world that He gave His only begotten Son that whosoever believes in him should not perish but have everlasting life." That is certainly a correct answer when we view the cross from God's viewpoint. Jesus made it clear throughout His ministry that He was going to the cross and sought to prepare His disciples to that end.

But why did the very ones He came to save crucify Him? The answer lies in several statements Jesus made. First of all, when standing before Pilate, Jesus referred to His kingdom.

Pilate immediately seized upon that statement by saying, "So you are a king?" Jesus answered, "You say correctly that I am a king. For this I have been born, and for this I have come into the world…" Here Jesus makes clear that He came not only as the Savior of the world but also to establish His kingdom.

Let's look at another statement. This time Jesus frames it in the form of a parable. We find it in Luke 19:11–14. Jesus tells of a certain nobleman who went into a distant country to receive a kingdom for himself. After leaving his servants, they sent a delegation after him saying, "We do not want this man to reign over us."

Although there is more to this parable than I am addressing, Jesus nevertheless reveals some profound and insightful truth that can easily escape our notice. The statement, "We will not have this man reign over us" is the very reason they later crucified Him.

There is a popular Christian song that begins "Everyone needs compassion…forgiveness… a Savior…" Yes, we all need a Savior, but how many want a Ruler? We welcome the Savior but resist Him as the Sovereign Lord. We will expound upon this later in the book.

CHAPTER EIGHT

What Did God Purchase?

And they sang a new song saying,
"Worthy art Thou to take the book, and to
break its seals; for Thou wast slain, and didst
purchase for God with Thy blood men from
every tribe and tongue and people and nation."
REVELATION 5:9

We now come to the focal point of this book. I'm going to share with you an illustration that I believe the Lord gave me shortly after I graduated from Bible college. Hopefully this illustration will help to shed some further light into the whole atoning work of the cross.

Imagine that my wife and I have been married for just one year. When we were first married, we both had debts over our heads and agreed that we were going to do everything possible to eliminate them. We both take on extra jobs by working in the evenings. Slowly but surely we are able to pay off every creditor, and by the time we reach our first anniversary, we are debt free and have a small nest egg of one thousand dollars.

We decide to celebrate our anniversary by going out to eat, something we refrained from doing during our days of debt. While enjoying our meal together, I suggest to my wife that we buy a car. We had been relying on public transport prior to this, as well as occasional help from our friends. My suggestion of buying a car brings an immediate reaction from my wife. She reminds me that we are not going back into debt, not even for a car. Agreeing with her, I suggest we use the thousand dollars we have set aside. My wife laughs and says, "You can't buy a car for a thousand dollars." After convincing her that all things are possible, I suggest she prays while I go car shopping.

For days I scour the newspapers as well as every possible car yard I can find. Finally a friend tips me off about a great deal he knows about. I set off, and sure enough, I find the perfect car for under one thousand dollars. The car is some twenty years old and has all the dust and dirt to prove it.

Here is where I need to leave the illustration of the car and insert something about my wife and myself. We are both clean freaks; we love cleanliness and order. In fact, we are known in the community as "Mr. and Mrs. Clean." While our home is quite modest, it is exceptionally clean and extremely tidy. We have been able to buy some great used furniture. Being handy with a paint brush, we have spruced up the house in a way that makes it look like a million dollars.

Soon after buying the car, I set about cleaning it. I gather together all the necessary cleaning gear, and the process begins. I first wash the car thoroughly with soap and water. I then use some type of solvent to remove the grease and grime the soap has failed to remove. Following that, I polish the car until it begins to look like new. Not content with having the car clean on the outside, I begin cleaning the inside. I first vacuum and shampoo the carpets. I then tackle the upholstery with the best upholstery cleaner I can find. The only thing left now to do are the windows and dash. After a good five hours of work, the car is immaculate. One would never guess it was so old. I've even steam cleaned the engine in case anyone looks under the hood.

After admiring my "new" car, I head into the house with all the cleaning paraphernalia in hand. I place everything I have used to clean the car on the kitchen table. I have numerous rags, sponges, and used paper towels, as well as a five-gallon pail of filthy, muddy water. I empty all the dust and debris out of the vacuum cleaner, piling it alongside the other cleaning materials. I then call my wife to come and see all that I have accomplished. Excitedly, she runs to the window to look out, but instead I call her to where I'm standing. Then, pointing to the kitchen table, I announce, "Look at what we were able to buy for one thousand dollars." She stares in disbelief at the pile of dirt, dust, and trash I'm pointing to. "You're crazy," she says. "What do you mean we got all this dirt for a thousand dollars? I thought you went to buy a car!"

While the illustration may not be perfect, it certainly helps us to focus on an important but long-neglected aspect of the cross.

Yes, the blood of Jesus Christ God's Son cleanses us from all sin. This was the good news proclaimed by the angel to Joseph: "And she shall bear a son, and you shall call His name Jesus, for it is He who will save His people from their sin." The New Testament abounds will similar verses concerning forgiveness from sin by the blood of Jesus.

But that is not all that Jesus sought to accomplish through His death. First of all, our sin has no value to God. According to the prophet Micah, God cast our sins into the depths of the sea, or as the Psalmist declares in Psalm 103:12, "As far as the East is from the West so far has He removed our transgressions from us." In other words, God has no use for our sin. God is not frantically looking all over creation for some rare sin to add to His collection the way some collectors adds stamps or coins to theirs. Our sins have no purpose whatsoever in God's economy. They can't preach, testify, prophesy, glorify, or do anything beneficial for God or His kingdom. They are mere garbage that has to be buried.

Then why did Christ die?

CHAPTER NINE

Four
New Testament
Images

But by His doing you are in Christ Jesus,
who became to us wisdom from God and
righteousness and sanctification, and redemption.

1 CORINTHIANS 1:30

The full scope of Christ's death is impossible to explain in just one word. The writers of the new Testament use a variety of words or images to sum up all that Christ accomplished on the cross.

In his wonderful book The Cross, John R. W. Stott elaborates on four images used in the New Testament to describe all that Christ accomplished in His atoning work. These are "propitiation," "redemption," "justification," and "reconciliation." Let's listen to what he says:

> As for the imagery, 'propitiation' introduces us to rituals at a shrine, 'redemption' to transactions in a market-place, 'justification' to proceedings in a law court, and 'reconciliation' to experiences in a home or family....
>
> We have examined four of the principal New Testament images of salvation, taken from the shrine [spiritual], the market [commercial], the law court [judicial], and the home [relational]. Words in brackets mine. Their pictorial nature makes it impossible to integrate them neatly with one another. Temple sacrifices and legal verdicts, the slave in the market and the child in the home all clearly belong to different worlds. Nevertheless certain themes emerge from all four images.
>
> First, each highlights a different aspect of our human need. Propitiation underscores the wrath of God upon us, redemption our captivity to sin, justification our guilt, and reconciliation our enmity against God and alienation from Him.

These metaphors do not flatter us. They expose the magnitude of our need.

Secondly, all four images emphasize that the saving initiative was taken by God in his love. It is he who has propitiated his own wrath, redeemed us from our miserable bondage, declared us righteous in his sight, and reconciled us to himself. Relevant texts leave us in no doubt about this; "God...so loved us, and sent his Son to be the propitiation for our sins,' 'God...has come and has redeemed his people.' 'It is God who justifies.' 'God... reconciled us to himself through Christ.'

Thirdly, all four images plainly teach that God's saving work was achieved through blood shedding, that is, the substitutionary sacrifice of Christ. With regard to the blood of Christ the texts are again unequivocal. 'God presented him as a propitiatory sacrifice through faith in his blood. 'In him we have redemption through his blood.' 'We have now been justified by his blood.' 'You who once were far away have been brought near (i.e. reconciled) through the blood of Christ.' Since Christ's blood is a symbol of his life laid down in violent death, it is also plain in each of the four images that he died in our place as our substitute. The death of Jesus was the atoning sacrifice by which God averted his wrath from us, the ransom-price by which we have been redeemed, the condemnation of the innocent that the guilty might be justified, and the sinless One being made sin for us.[6]

Stott's entire 350-page book is based entirely on the cross. I highly recommend it to you.

In a similar way Leon Morris in his book, The Cross in the New Testament; writes:

> Our survey of the doctrine throughout the New Testament has uncovered a bewildering variety of ways of looking at Christ's work. Redemption, for example, is a figure derived from the slave market or the freeing of prisoners of war. It has to do with setting the captives free on payment of price. Justification is a legal metaphor. It interprets salvation through the law court and sees it as a verdict of acquittal. Reconciliation refers to the making up after a quarrel, the doing away of a state of hostility. Propitiation has to do with anger. It reminds us of the wrath of God exercised toward every evil thing and also of the fact that Christ has removed that wrath. How are these theories to be gathered together under one theory? It cannot be done…but the fact is that it is too great in extent and too complex in character for us to comprehend it all in one theory.[7]

By far the most familiar and popular "image" for most Christians is that of justification. It is the image of redemption. However, that is largely neglected and almost totally misunderstood and applied.

This will be our theme in the next chapter.

[6] John Stott, *The Cross* (Downers Grove, IL: InterVarsity Press, 1986), 167.

[7] Leon Morris, *The Cross in the New Testament* (Exeter: The Paternoster Press, 1999), 339.

Four New Testament Images

CHAPTER TEN

Redemption

Knowing that you were not redeemed with
perishable things like silver and gold from your
futile way of life inherited from your forefathers
but with precious blood, as of a lamb unblemished
and spotless, the blood of Christ.

1 PETER 1:19-20

The aspect of redemption has been attacked more than any other image used to describe our "so great salvation." Here is what the great Charles Spurgeon said in this regard:

> Attacks have often been made upon the central doctrine of the gospel, namely the doctrine of redemption or atonement…these onslaughts have in many instances been very craftily made; they have professed to be mere corrections of our phraseology, but were essential assaults upon the truth itself. We believe that in and through the blood of Jesus we have redemption and that we have been ransomed from destruction by the Mediator's death, the Lord Jesus having bought us by the suit and service which He rendered in our place and stead…There may have been among us certain persons who carried ideas of the shop and the counter into their notion of redemption, but we maintain that even these were nearer the truth than those who reduce the ransom paid by the Lord Jesus to nothing, and make his redemption a meaningless figure of speech…Paul however was not afraid of the mercantile theory, if so men please to call it, for he writes. "Ye were bought." Yea, to make it still more sure he puts it, "bought with a price." If it means anything it must mean that a price was paid for us…"

Part of the confusion regarding redemption revolves around the question to who was the price paid to? Some suggest that Jesus, through His death, paid the devil for our release. But no price was ever paid to the devil. We were never the rightful possession of Satan even though we were under his evil power. Perhaps the story of Israel's release from bondage best describes the sinners relationship to the devil. When God delivered Israel from Egypt He did not pay Pharaoh for their release. They were set free both by the power of God, as well as the blood of the lamb. The blood was the price paid for their deliverance and cleansing.[8]

Spurgeon explains it this way.

There was a time brethren when we thought ourselves to be our own. Why? "Because ye were bought with a price." Bought from whom? May I not fairly say that, in one sense, you were bought from yourselves? Where else is the force of expression, "Ye are not your own." Through the redemption which is in Christ Jesus a compensation had been given to you for yourselves, so that your rights to yourself are now the property of the Lord Jesus. That independence and liberty that you once delighted in is now surrendered...Our vested interest in ourselves, though it never was a true property at all, is once for all surrendered to him who laid down His life for us.[9]

Here is how Gordon Watt in his book, *The Meaning Of The Cross* explains what being bought with a price means.

Now let me turn to the second imperative, which is the imperative claim of the cross, 1 Corinthians 6:20, "For ye are bought with a price: therefore glorify God in your body, and in your spirit, which are God's." The reason for this claim is that we are bought. Now on everything that is yours you have a claim. If you go into a store and buy something, three things at least you expect to get; first, value for your money; second, some service out of what you purchase, and third, some pleasure out of it. If you do not get those three things you have made a very poor buy, haven't you? I wonder if any of us are poor bargains to the Lord Jesus Christ. I wonder if any of us have been proving that for all practical purposes Christ has died in vain for us.

What is the price that He paid for us? Calvary and all that means in laying down His life, in yielding Himself into the hands of wicked men, in surrendering Himself to do the will of God. That is the price He has paid for us. What is the purpose for which the price has been paid? That we might glorify God. That we might glorify God in our bodies and in our spirits, which are His: that is to say, in the outer and inner life; in the activities of the mind and body as well as in the attitude of heart and spirit; in public life and in private life; in the place where the eyes of others are upon us and in the place where no eye is on us except the eye of God. In yielding to God for this end we do want to remember that it is only honest and honorable to do so, because, body and spirit, are His.

Calvary claims the whole man, because Calvary proclaims that the whole man has been purchased.

Do not let any of us imagine that there can be dual sovereignty in our lives, Christ and something else. Christ never goes halves with anything or with any one; it is all or nothing. That is the claim that He makes, and when you respond to that claim… you will find that everything in life falls into its right place.[10]

Allow me to share my personal testimony at this point. I was raised in a godly home. My father was a well-known and respected preacher with an international ministry. My dad was of the old school and would often preach on hell or at least mention it in his messages. So from my earliest recollection, I was made aware of the fact that hell was a real place. I have no distinct memory of ever accepting Christ into my life as a child. However, around my early teen years, I began to realize my need of a Savior. Many times I would find myself literally shaking under conviction of sin knowing that I was hell bound if I didn't repent and turn to God. This continued for several years as I steadfastly resisted the convicting of the Holy Spirit.

I need to add something here. I was the middle child, with an older and younger brother on either side. Both my brothers were extremely bright and excelled in school. For whatever reason, I was the one who struggled and detested going to school. On more than one occasion I failed and had the F on my report card to prove it. While both my brothers were academically gifted, I excelled in the area of art. I loved to draw and had a creative bent. It was my art that I lived for. At least I could hold my own against my brothers in this regard. As a young teen, I made up my mind that I would pursue a career in art. This was my comfort zone and one in which I felt loved and accepted.

During my final year of high school, I once more came under conviction during a Sunday evening service. My resistance prior to this lay in the fact that I was not prepared to give God my life. I realized my need of a Savior but didn't like the idea of someone telling me what to do. After all, I had plans, and nobody was going to interfere with them. At least that was my mindset at the time. I was more than willing to give God my sin and longed for forgiveness and the assurance of salvation. The real struggle I had was, what if God had other plans for my life? Was I prepared to give God everything, not simply my past but also my future?

That night I found my way to the altar and began to pray. My prayer was simple yet sincere. It went something like this, as I recall: "Lord, I'm asking You for forgiveness. I've sinned and need Your grace. Please cleanse me of all the things I've done; I'm truly sorry. But Lord, I'm not just asking for forgiveness. I'm here to ask You to become Lord of my life. I surrender to You my life. All my plans, dreams, and desires I give to You. Do with me whatever You see fit to do. Amen."

A short time after making that commitment, I opened my Bible to 1 Corinthians 6:19–20 and read: "Or do you not know that your body is a temple of the Holy Spirit who is in you, whom you have from God, and that you are not your own? For you have been bought with a price: therefore glorify God in your body." Notice if you will Paul's emphasis on the word "body." It is your body that God is after. As I mentioned earlier, our sin is of no value to God. We were created by Him and for Him. It was to this end that Christ died, that He might redeem for Himself what He originally created for Himself.

No one portion of Scripture should be used to establish doctrine. To use these verses by themselves would only serve to weaken my argument. We are told, "In the multitude of witnesses there is safety" or "In the mouth of two or three witnesses let every word be established." Therefore, it is necessary to look at other passages that support this image of redemption.

In Paul's letter to Titus, he states, "Looking for the blessed hope and the appearing of the glory of our great God and Savior, Jesus Christ, who gave Himself for us, that he might redeem us from every lawless deed and purify for Himself a people for His own possession, zealous for good deeds" (Titus 2:13–14). Here Paul deals with what I tend to address as the two sides of the cross. Picture, if you will, the cross. On the left side we have Christ dying for our sins. This is the aspect of the cross that we are most familiar with. On this side of the cross we have forgiveness of sin. We have peace with God as well as the peace of God. Here we are reconciled to God and become sons and daughters whereby we cry, "Abba Father." This is the aspect of the cross that we tend to emphasize the most because without it there is no forgiveness of sin. Now I have no desire to diminish the importance of this aspect in any way. The Scriptures abound with verses that support this aspect of teaching. Paul, though, does not put a period after, "That He might redeem us from every lawless deed" but continues on with and "purify for Himself a people for His own possession…"

We could say that one side of the cross refers to what Christ did for us, while the other side of the cross deals with what Christ did for God. In other words, what the blood cleanses on one side, the blood claims on the other side. Failure to teach or preach both of these aspects will ultimately lead to error. On one side we see Christ as Savior and on the other as Sovereign. On one side we have His kindness manifested but on the other side, His kingship or lordship over us.

Allow me to underscore two words from these two verses—people and possession. The object of Christ's suffering was to ultimately restore a people to and for Himself. We have tended to place the emphasis on sin and leave it there, but what God had in mind was to redeem for Himself a people for His own possession. This takes us back to the "beginning" where we read that "all things were created by Him and for Him. You are not your own you have been bought with a price…"

Charles Spurgeon elaborates on this by saying:

I will mention a fifth pair of contrasts: Submission and Expectancy. These are both suggested by my text. Submission: "Ye are not your own" and therefore God has a right to do whatever he wills with you…if He says, "Migrate across the seas; go to a new country, cut every tie and break the fondest connections," you must cheerfully obey, for "ye are not your own." If the call of duty should be to "Go, preach the gospel among the heathen; go and die among them; find a grave where malaria shortens life, or cruelty brings sudden death"; you must go without question, for "ye are not your own." Ours is not to raise questions or debates, for those can only be legitimate among persons who are their own.

Spurgeon then goes on to speak about expectancy:

A piece of clay that lies in the pit all its own has no destiny before it, but when it has been purchased by the potter, and beaten and prepared, and when it feels itself revolving on the wheel, it has just reason to believe it will bear a useful part in time to come. It might say if it could speak. "I am not my own lump of clay I have been bought with a great price, and therefore something is to be made of me. It doth not yet appear what I shall be, but when he that fashioneth hath finished me I shall, no doubt, be worthy of the hand that has wrought this upon me." Raise your expectations as high as ever you will, God meaneth to do for you exceeding abundantly above what you can ask or even think... (Eph. 3:20)

One of the great lies of the devil is to have us believe that if we truly surrender everything to God, we will suffer immeasurable consequences. Nothing could be further from the truth. Jesus made it abundantly clear that "If you seek to save your life you will lose it but if you lose it you will find it." Since God has created us for Himself, we will never find true meaning in life until we die to self and live for Him alone. I believe there are tens of millions of Christians who live lives of total frustration because they have never really given themselves unreservedly to God. They readily accept Him as Savior but refuse to acknowledge Him as Lord.

Today we have watered the gospel down to an irresistible offer of eternal life, without any conditions whatsoever. This cheapening of the grace of God is what I believe Jude had in mind when he began his epistle with an appeal to "contend earnestly for the faith which was once for all delivered to the saints. For certain persons have crept in unnoticed, those who were long beforehand marked out for this condemnation, ungodly persons who turn the grace of God into licentiousness and deny the only Master and Lord, Jesus Christ" (Jude 3–4).

Jude carried a genuine burden and concern in his day for what he saw to be a major departure from the faith as it was first delivered to the saints. His burden was twofold: an incorrect teaching regarding grace and a denial of Jesus as Master and Lord. I believe these two are inseparably joined together. If Christ is not given His rightful place as Lord, then we will continue to indulge our self-life with whatever we think best. Or as Paul puts it in writing to the Romans, "Are we to continue in sin that grace may abound? May it never be!"

Our study continues on this theme of "redemption" by looking at other passages along this line. In Paul's letter to the Romans he writes, "For to this end Christ died and lived again, that He might be Lord both of the dead and the living." Here Paul clearly reveals to us the reason Christ died. Notice he does not say that Christ died to be our Savior but our Lord (Rom. 14:9). Obviously there can be no regeneration without a Savior, but we need to keep in mind that "God hath made Him both Lord and Christ—this Jesus whom you crucified." We do not have the prerogative to choose whether we will have Jesus as our Savior or as our Lord. As the old saying goes, "If He is not Lord of all, He is not Lord at all."

Today the emphasis on lordship has virtually been eliminated from our preaching and teaching. We tend to emphasize what Christ has done for us rather than His claim over us. Only this morning I found myself singing one of Fanny Crosby's hymns, "Redeemed." Listen to what she wrote:

> Redeemed, how I love to proclaim it!
> Redeemed by the blood of the Lamb;
> Redeemed through His infinite mercy,
> His child and forever I am.
> (Fanny J. Crosby 1820-1915).

Most of the old hymn writers understood and underscored the importance of Christ's ownership over us. Pick up any hymnal and look under the topic of the atonement and you will find numerous examples of hymns exalting Christ as Lord.

Returning to our passage in Romans 14:7–9, J. Gregory Mantle in his book *The Counterfeit Christ* writes:

No words could express more plainly than these that the purpose of Christ's death and resurrection was to win undisputed Lordship over man. "To this end"—so the passage reads in the Authorized Version—"To this end," and no other; "for this purpose," and nothing short of it, He died on the cross of Calvary. He rose from the dead, and lives a life on which the tooth of time has no power, in order to execute that Lordship. Therefore to dispute His Sovereignty, to deny His Lordship, is to rob Him of the fruit of His passion.

Among the most honored names in the United States is that of Wendell Phillips the incorruptible orator and statesman. He was one of the most gifted of men. He did possibly more than any other man to strike the shackles from four million slaves. He is known to this day as "the Boston Orator…the man who could not be bought." Shortly before he died, he was asked by a friend whether there was any crisis in his life that explained his unfaltering devotion to his Master. This is what he said: "When I was fourteen, I heard Lyman Beecher preach on the Lordship of Jesus Christ. I went to my room, locked the door and then threw myself on the floor of the room. This was what I said: 'O God, I belong to Thee; take what is Thine own; I gladly recognize Thy ownership in me; I now take Thee as my Lord and Master.' From that time to this I have never known a thing to be wrong without having an aversion to it; and I have never seen anything to be right without having an attraction to it."

Many are happy to take life from Jesus Christ who hesitate to take law from Him. But there can be no real loyalty unless we make Him the Lord of our conduct as well as the Savior of our soul. How was it that Wendell Phillips was able to make that remarkable statement about aversion and attraction? Having made Jesus Lord, everything was changed. His Master stood by him in every conflict; He gave him strength for every task; He defined for him all his duties; He rejoiced in all his victories. Christ had become his Comrade, and the fully surrendered man found himself under the government of a higher will than his own, for he now had a Ruler as well as a Savior.[11]

Mantle continues on in the same message to say:

There is a place in your heart called a throne. Someone always occupies that place. The rival claimants are Christ and Self. Which of these is on the throne? Christ will brook no rival. He will accept no divided allegiance. So long as one apartment is withheld. He will not assume control…. Jesus asks for the ownership of the entire being, for the whole is His by creative and redemptive right, and till all is yielded there is discord and disharmony…When we can say: "The government is on His shoulders," then every part of the little kingdom acknowledges His Kingship and rejoices in His Sovereignty. It was for this man was created; it was for this Jesus died and rose again.[12]

Oswald Chambers, better known for his devotional book *My Utmost for His Highest*, defines "redemption" as follows:

"The meaning of Redemption is not simply the regeneration of individuals, but that the whole human race is rehabilitated, put back to where God designed it to be…"

Notice, if you will, how these older writers and preachers tied the atoning work of Christ to creation. As I stated in the first few chapters, we can never understand the cross until we grasp the mind of God as it relates to His original purpose. Once again, the cross is God's medicine for man's sickness. The essence of man's sickness is that of "self."

We will continue this in the next chapter.

[8] Charles H. Spurgeon. Metropolitan Tabernacle Pulpit, message title *Redemption By Price*, Vol. 26. (Pasadena, TX: Pilgrim Publications, 1971), 469.

[9] Ibid.

[10] Rev. Gordon Watt, *The Meaning Of The Cross* (Dorset, England: The Overcomer Literature Trust, 1939), 96.

[11] J. Gregory Mantle. *The Counterfeit Christ*. (Harrisburg, PA: Christian Publications, Inc., 1968) 120–21.

[12] Ibid.

Redemption

CHAPTER ELEVEN

Blood Bought

But false prophets also arose among the people,
just as there will also be false teachers among you,
who will secretly introduce destructive heresies,
even denying the Master who bought them...

2 PETER 2:1

W e want to continue our study of this wonderful and yet often overlooked word *redemption*. Paul, in his letter to the Ephesians, uses the word twice within the first chapter. In verse seven, he uses the word in regard to what has already been accomplished when he writes, "In Him we have redemption through His blood, the forgiveness of our trespasses, according to the riches of His grace." Paul then goes on to explain in verses 13 and 14 what remains to take place: "...having also believed you were sealed in Him with the Holy Spirit of promise, who is given as a pledge of our inheritance, with a view to the redemption of God's own possession, to the praise of His glory." Here is how the *Pulpit Commentary* explains it:

> The 'purchased possession' are the possessors of the inheritance. It is a theocratic word that was well understood. It was used to describe ancient Israel as property which the Lord had acquired for Himself. We Christians now answer to the ancient designation. We are the successors of Israel, and therefore the Lord claims us as a people for His peculiar possession (1 Peter 2:9). We are the peculiar property of God by right of redemption. [12]

> In Ellicott's commentary, he says, "The original word here rendered 'purchased possession' properly means 'the act of purchase or acquisition.'"[13]

By far one of the clearest examples of this is found in John's glorious vision recorded in the book of Revelation. In the fifth chapter, John describes how he feels when he sees in the right hand of Him who sat on the throne a book sealed with seven seals. The angel calls out, "Who is worthy to open the book and to break the seals?" John begins to weep as no one was found worthy. Then one of the elders says to him, "Stop weeping; behold the Lion that is from the tribe of Judah, the Root of David has overcome, so as to open the book and its seven seals." John looks and sees "a Lamb standing as if slain…" As soon as the Lord takes the book, heaven erupts in song. Here is what they sang: "Worthy art Thou to take the book, and to break its seals; for Thou wast slain, and did purchase for God with Thy blood men from every tribe and tongue and people and nation."

John reveals to us the "heavenly viewpoint" as to why Christ died. He was slain in order to purchase for God with His blood…men. In other words, the cross was ultimately about God and not man. We have focused on ourselves as the focal point of Christ's death and resurrection, but here we see that it was really all for God's sake. Yes, we were forgiven through His blood and yes, we were reconciled and became sons and daughters, etc., but the Son did it all for the Father. He purchased us for God. Do you see it? "All things were created by Him and for Him" (Col. 1:16). "We are His people and the sheep of His pasture" (Ps. 79:13). "The earth is the Lord's and the fullness thereof" (Ps. 24:1).

Listen to what Spurgeon writes on this passage:

In heaven they adore the Lord as their Redeemer. "Thou wast slain, and hast redeemed us to God by Thy blood." The metaphor of redemption, if I understand it, signifies this. A thing which is redeemed in the strict sense belonged beforehand to the person who redeemed it. Under Jewish law lands were mortgaged as they are now; and when the money lent upon them, or the service due to them was paid, the land was said to be redeemed. An inheritance first belonged to a person, and then went away from him by stress of poverty, but if a certain price was paid, it came back. Now "all souls are mine" saith the Lord, and the souls of men belong to the Lord. The metaphor is used, and, mark, these expressions are but metaphors; but the sense under them is no metaphor; it is fact. Our souls had come under mortgage, as it were, through the sin committed, so that God could not accept us without violating His justice until something had been done by which He who is infinitely just could freely distribute His grace to us... "The Lord's portion is His people;" that portion was hampered until Jesus set us free. We were God's always, but we had fallen into slavery to sin. Jesus came to make recompense for our offenses, and thus we return to where we were before. ...They are redeemed, and they are redeemed unto God. That is the point: they come back to God as lands come back to the owner when the mortgage is discharged. We come back to God again, to whom we always and ever did belong, because Jesus has redeemed us to God by His blood.[14]

While we have been centering our thoughts on passages from the New Testament, we also want to explore redemption from the Old Testament as well. Before we do this, however, I want to look at another passage, this time from Peter's second epistle beginning in verse 1. Here we find Peter warning the church regarding a coming problem. He begins by referring to the fact that they have had some false prophets that have caused them trouble in the past. Now he seeks to warn them of an impending threat from false teachers. The difficulty that they are about to face lies in the fact that these teachers will come in secret.

When something is done in secret, we are not aware of it most of the time. I recall when my wife and I were serving the Lord in Papua, New Guinea, in the early 1970s. We were living in the capital city of Port Moresby at the time. The area where we lived had had a number of break ins. Our car had been stolen one night, and so we were extremely careful to make sure our home was locked and secure before going to bed at night. We were concerned not only for our own safety but also for the safety of our two young daughters. One morning as I made my way down the hall from our bedroom into the living room, I noticed that the front door was wide open. At first I couldn't believe it, as nothing appeared to be out of order. Thinking that I had failed to shut it properly the night before, I closed it and headed into the kitchen. It was only then that I realized that we had had some intruders, as the kitchen door also was wide open. My first concern was for our children. Thankfully they were still in their beds fast asleep. As I began to make my way back through the house, I returned to our bedroom to discover that someone had stolen our tape recorder, which was plugged in directly below my wife's pillow. Then I noticed that my wallet was missing from the side table beside our bed. All of this took place while we were asleep. It happened secretly. We were totally unaware of it until it was too late.

This is the way Peter relays his warning to the church. These false teachers will come in secretly. He then goes on to warn them that they will introduce "destructive heresies" or "damnable doctrines." These are strong words indeed. Peter is no doubt trying to emphasize to the Church the danger of these teachings they are about to encounter. In order to stress the seriousness of his concern, he writes that they will even "deny the Master who bought them."

When I first became aware of this verse, I could hardly believe what I had just read. Out of all the things that Peter could have written about false teaching, he chooses to focus on denying the Master who bought them. (Could it be that Peter was still shamefully aware of his own denial of his Lord and Master following Christ's arrest in the garden?)

Today this would not be considered false teaching, as we have come to accept it as the norm. After all, who places any emphasis on lordship these days? We tend to tout a message of grace that comes with no strings attached. Lordship is presented as some sort of optional extra that you can have if you want to but is really not necessary.

The phrase "the Master who bought them" obviously refers to the redeeming work of Christ. But here Peter refers to Him as Master. Master conveys ownership. How was this ownership obtained? By purchase. "He bought them."

Allow me to insert here a portion of a message given by the great Alexander Maclaren and taken from Expositions of Holy Scriptures. Maclaren is expounding this very passage in 2 Peter 2:

> The word that is here rendered rightly enough 'Lord' is the word which has been transferred into English as 'despots' and it carries with it some suggestion of the roughness and absoluteness of authority which that word suggests to us. It does not mean merely master, it means 'owner.' And it suggests an unconditional authority, to which the only thing in us that corresponds is abject and unconditional submission. That is what Christ is to you and me; the Lord, the Despot, the Owner.
>
> But we have not only the owner and slave here; we have one of the ugliest features of the institution referred to. You have the slave market, 'the Lord that bought them,' and because He purchased them, owns them. Think of the hell of miseries that are connected with that practice of buying and selling human flesh, and then estimate the magnificent boldness of the metaphor which Peter does not scruple (hesitate) to take from it here, speaking of the owner who acquired them by a price. And not only that, but slaves will run away, and when they are stopped, and asked who they belong to, will say they know nothing about him. And so here is the runaway's denial, 'denying the Lord that bought them.'...Did it ever occur to you what a pathetic force there is in Peter's picking out

that word 'denying' as the shorthand expression for all sorts of sins? Who was it that thrice denied that he knew Him? That expression went very deep into the Apostle; and here as I take it, is a most significant illustration of his penitent remembrance of his past life, all the more significant because of its reticence. The allusion is one that nobody could catch that did not know his past, but which to those who did know, it was full of meaning and of pathos:—Denying the Lord, as I did on that dismal morning, in the High Priest's palace. I am speaking about it, for I know what it comes to and the tears that will follow after.[15]

Are you beginning to see the importance of this term redemption? Is it any wonder, then, that the enemy has secretly crept into the Church and gradually but systematically eliminated this type of doctrine? The enemy is a formidable foe and will do anything and everything within his power to deceive us into thinking that we simply give Christ our sins and receive forgiveness, yet deny Him as our Master and Lord.

Undoubtedly this gives the enemy the upper hand. If he can convince us to do that which is right in our own eyes instead of surrendering our lives in total consecration to God, then he has nothing to worry about. He can go about establishing his kingdom without the slightest concern from his archrival—God.

You may recall the story of the Philistines who over a period of time went throughout the nation of Israel destroying the blacksmiths' shops. Israel's economy was agriculturally based. The people were dependent on the blacksmiths for their various agricultural implements like axes, hoes, plowshares, forks, etc. Israel, as a result, became entirely dependent upon the Philistines for repairing their broken tools. The Philistines established a fixed charge for every tool they repaired. While that presented a real problem for the Israelites, the Philistines had a far more sinister scheme in mind.

We read in 1 Samuel 13:19 that the real reason behind destroying the blacksmith shops was "lest the Hebrews make swords and spears." You see, the blacksmith shops were not only the place where the agricultural implements were made but also the place where the weapons of war were forged. In verse 22 we read, "So it came about on the day of battle that neither sword nor spear were found in the hands of any of the people…" Israel was defenseless on the day of battle.

I believe that long ago the devil concocted a plan to eliminate the teaching of lordship from the Church, knowing that in the day of battle God would stand alone, stripped of His rightful army that He had relied upon to do His will. Do you recall the response of those who were to be part of His Kingdom? "We will not have this man rule over us." J. Gregory Mantle states it this way:

> The question of authority has become one of the gravest questions. Never was there such a wide spread revolt against all rightful authority as today… All living things need a ruling force. The body is useless and immediately plays the fool without a head to

direct its movements. An army is powerless when there is no supreme commander to issue orders. If these things are true in the lowest realms, how much more important is the question of authority when we speak of our relationship to our Lord. A true Christian is a man or woman under the authority of the Lord Jesus Christ.[16]

---

[13] Charles John Ellicott, *Ellicott's Commentary. Book of Ephesians* by the Right Rev. Alfred Barry D.D. (Grand Rapids, MI: Zondervan Publishing House, 1981).

[14] Charles Spurgeon. *Metropolitan Tabernacle Pulpit*, Message title: "Jesus, the Delight Of Heaven." Vol. 21. (Pasadena, TX: Pilgrim Publications, 1971), 1975.

[15] Alexander Maclaren, *Expositions of Holy Scriptures*, Vol. 16. (Ada, MI: Baker Book House, 1978), 216.

[16] Mantle, *The Counterfeit Christ*, 117.

Blood Bought

CHAPTER TWELVE

Your Life is Just a Vapor

Yet you do not know what your life will be like tomorrow. You are just a vapor that appears for a little while and then vanishes away.

JAMES 4:14

W e have been looking into the significance of the word redemption. In this chapter we want to apply this doctrine in a practical way to our lives. Virtually every American young person during their final years of high school is faced with the question, "What next?" Most of us rely upon the help of our parents, friends, or school counselors to guide us as to our next move. For most the choice is to either join the workforce or apply to some college with the hope of earning a degree. Usually the person with a college degree will secure a better job and higher salary. The temptation of receiving a higher salary is the main motivation in going to college. After all, a higher salary usually translates into having a better standard of living, not to mention the "toys" that go with it. Who doesn't want to live in an upscale neighborhood, dress well, drive a flashy car, and be able to dine out whenever and wherever one chooses? This we refer to as the American dream. It has become our right, or so we are taught.

While some are slow to find their niche, others dream of achieving their goals while still quite young. My goal, as I have told you, was to become a graphic artist. For another it may be to become a physician, dentist, lawyer, pilot, accountant, or politician. The list is endless.

James in his short epistle seems to capture and challenge this process of finding the right career. In 4:13–17 he writes, "Come now you who say, today or tomorrow we will go into such a city, and spend a year there and engage in business and make a profit."

James describes a person who knows what he dreams of doing with his life. In this case, he has assessed his situation and concluded that he has little, if any, opportunity for advancement where he lives. In order to realize his goals, he is prepared to leave and move to another city. His plans are to become a businessman and turn a profit.

Now on the surface you can't criticize such a plan. This person is not planning some illegal activity in order to make money. There is no suggestion of drug smuggling or some other unethical endeavor. Instead he plans to make money by starting some type of business.

Most of us can relate to this. We have followed a similar path. For some you can look back and recall the years you spent working toward your degree. You can remember your first paycheck, apartment, car, etc. What sets this young person apart is that he is born again. This is clearly implied in the context of these verses.

I like to imagine that this young person was raised in the local church and attended the youth group. When the decision is made to leave home, church, and perhaps family, this young person makes the rounds of saying good-bye to everyone he knows and loves. The last person he needs to say good-bye to is his pastor. In this case, the pastor is James. While excitedly explaining his plans and dreams to become a businessman to his pastor, he pauses momentarily.

Pastor James, who has been waiting for such an opportunity, begins to explain to him the brevity of life. "You are just a vapor that appears for a little while and then vanishes away." Like most young people, he assumes he will live forever, and he has never taken account of how short life really is. Job states, "Our days are swifter than a weaver's shuttle" (Job 7:6). In yet another place Job writes, "Now my days are swifter than a runner; they flee away, they see no good. They slip by like reed boats, like an eagle that swoops on its prey" (Job 9:25-26). I can testify to the speed at which life passes. It seems only yesterday that I was completing college and wondering what the future had in store. Now in my late sixties I look back in amazement at how time passes.

James uses the analogy of a vapor to illustrate how quickly life passes. We have all experienced setting off to school or work, only to discover that there is a heavy mist enveloping everything we can see. Carefully we make our way through it, thinking to ourselves it will be gone in a few hours. Sure enough, by the time we return home, the mist has evaporated and is no more. Life, James says, is just like that—here one minute and gone the next. James then challenges this person with the words, "Instead you ought to say, if the Lord wills, we shall live and also do this or that."

The question James raises is whether this young person has sought the will of God. "If the Lord wills." As Christians, we have no right to determine what we will do with our lives. We are "not our own," and therefore, we are not free to make our own decisions and plans. The will of God is the paramount issue that every believer has to settle.

James refuses to back down and continues, "But as it is, you boast in your arrogance. All such boasting is evil." I like the way Eugene Peterson paraphrases this in his Message:

> And now I have a word for you who brashly announce, 'Today—at the latest tomorrow—we're off to such and such a city for the year. We're going to

start a business and make a lot of money. You don't know the first thing about tomorrow. You're nothing but a wisp of fog catching a brief bit of sun before disappearing. Instead make it a habit to say, if the Master wills it and we're still alive, we'll do this or that. As it is, you are full of your grandiose selves. All such vaunting self-importance is evil. In fact, if you know the right thing to do and don't do it, that, for you, is evil.

I don't think I would be far off the mark to say that 80 percent of all believers have never seriously given their lives to God. I can only imagine what would happen if we truly heeded this admonition to make it a habit to ask our Master for His will for our lives. Here again I would like to quote from Alexander Maclaren:

And so I come with this question: Do you, dear friend, day by day, yield to the absolute Master this absolute submission? And is that rebellious will— which is in you, as it is in us all—tamed and submitted so as that you can say, 'Speak, Lord! Thy servant heareth. Is it?" Further, the owner has the right, as part of that absolute authority of which I have been speaking, to settle without appeal each man's work... Jesus Christ has the right to regulate your life in all its details, to set you your tasks. Some of us will get what the world vulgarly calls 'more important duties;' some will get what the world ignorantly calls more 'insignificant' ones. What does that matter? It was the Owner who set us to our work... Again, the owner has the absolute right of possession of all the slave's possessions. And the owner has another right. He can say, 'Take the man's child and sell him in the market!' He can break up the family ties and separate husband and wife, and parent and child, and not a word can be said. Blessed they who can say, 'It is the Lord! Let Him do what seemeth Him good.' ...I can understand the vehement antagonism that some people have to Christ and Christianity, but what I cannot understand is the attitude of the immense mass of people that come to services like this, profess to believe that Jesus Christ's love for them brought Him to the cross, and yet will not even pay the poor tribute of a little interest and a momentary inclination of heart towards Him. 'Is it nothing to you, all you that pass by,' that Jesus Christ died for you? He bought you for His own. Let me beseech you to 'yield yourselves' servants, slaves of Christ, and then you will be free, and you will hear Him say in the very depth of your hearts, 'Henceforth I call you not slaves, but friends.'[17]

Paul the apostle was one of the most amazing men in history. Prior to having a meeting place with God, he sought to wreak havoc throughout the fledgling Church world. Saul (Paul) was a persecutor and valiant aggressor, according to his own testimony. It was Paul who consented to Stephen's stoning as well as the imprisonment of numerous believers. One day this fiery zealot was heading out on his mission to persecute the Church. He was clutching the very papers that gave him authority to carry out his work. While on the road to Damascus, he had an encounter with the living God. Blinded by the Shekinah glory of God, he fell to the ground and cried out, "What shall I do, Lord?"

Paul immediately recognized that he was now under God's authority. He didn't reply by saying, "Savior, thank you for saving me." This obviously marked the beginning of his conversion experience. He was in this moment aware of God's awesome power and authority. It transcended that of all earthly authority, and he immediately bowed in submission. "Lord" is the only correct response. But you can't say Lord without being willing to do what He says. Jesus said, "You call me Lord, Lord, but do not do the things that I say."

My father use to say we sing more lies on a Sunday morning than most of us tell throughout the rest of the year. How true. We stand and raise our hands while singing:

> *He is Lord, He is Lord,*
> *He has risen from the dead*
> *And He is Lord.*
> *Every knee will bow* (except mine)
> *Every tongue confess.*
> *That Jesus Christ is Lord.*

Do we really mean what we say? Or are we simply mouthing words that are not backed by our actions?

Before closing this chapter, allow me to direct your attention to another insightful verse of Scripture from Paul's letter to the Corinthians. In 2 Corinthians 5:15, Paul gives us the reason behind Jesus's death: "He died for all, that they who live should no longer live for themselves, but for Him who died and rose again on their behalf."

Nothing could be clearer than this: the cross was to radically change our entire life and purpose. Prior to the cross, we were consumed with doing our own thing. Life revolved around ourselves and our interests and desires. "All we like sheep had gone astray, we had turned every man to his own way." (Isa. 53:6) To truly understand and apply the cross to our lives means that we are to die to self and live solely for God. Just as our former life was used in selfish pursuits, so likewise our new life in Christ is to be lived for His pleasure and purpose. Paul testified, "We have as our ambition, whether at home or absent, to be pleasing unto Him" (2 Cor. 5:9).

Death to self is not a popular message these days. Books dealing with this topic just don't sell. A vast variety of books in Christian bookstores deal with self-improvement; topics range from weight loss to dressing for success and everything in between. We would far rather go to the beautician for a makeover than to the mortician for burial. We have become intoxicated with ourselves. Pastors these days spend more time in counseling than in sermon preparation. Hours if not weeks are spent trying to free someone from their past mistakes, and yet a simple trip to the cross will take care of that. Dead people don't have issues!

[17] Maclaren, *Expositions of Holy Scriptures*, 218.

Your Life is Just a Vapor

CHAPTER THIRTEEN

In Whom We Have Redemption Through His Blood

In Him we have redemption through His blood,

the forgiveness of our trespasses,

according to the riches of His grace.

EPHESIANS 1:7

J ust as the emphasis on "death to self" has all but been eliminated from our pulpits, so also has the mention of "blood." Many consider it too macabre or gruesome for people to deal with. Some time ago I was talking to a former Christian recording artist. He not only sang but also wrote many of his own songs. He told me that the CEO of his recording label had discouraged him from writing and recording songs that mentioned the blood of Christ.

Failure to understand the cost of our redemption will lead to a lack of appreciation as well as dedication to the very one who paid the supreme price for us. In his book Cross-Examined, author Mark Meynell writes:

> What few people acknowledge is that the creator of the universe has put a value on each human being that far exceeds anything the world has to offer. This is how the apostle Peter describes what has happened to a Christian: "for you know that it was not with perishable things such as silver or gold that you were redeemed from the empty way of life handed down to you from your forefathers, but with the precious blood of Christ, a lamb without blemish or defect" (1 Peter 1:18–19). Paul says something similar: In Him we have redemption through his blood, the forgiveness of sins (Ephesians 1:7). That is how much God values His human creatures. For Him, the shed blood of his Son was the price worth paying. That is the extent of His love, and at its heart is this idea of redemption.

He continues:

Redemption would have had another connotation for the original readers of the New Testament: the world of the slave auction. It is an alien world to us, full of injustice and horrific cruelty, but it was a fact of life two millennia ago. A slave was a person's property and a price needed to be paid for his or her life—a ransom, if you like. Imagine, a slave owner visiting the auction. Suppose he has become a Christian since selling off his former slaves. When he realizes that their condition has significantly deteriorated, he decides to buy them back for the express purpose of improving their lot. That "buying back" of what was originally his is redemption.[19]

While the author's illustration is somewhat flawed, nevertheless it helps to convey a little of what Jesus did for us. Jesus did not simply fork over a certain amount of money in order to redeem us, but rather "gave his life a ransom for many."

Spurgeon in his own masterful way describes the blood shedding of our Lord in this way:

There was a blood shedding once, that did all other shedding of blood by far out vie; (exceed or surpass) it was a man—a God—that shed his blood at that memorial season. Come and see it. Here is a garden, dark and gloomy; the ground is crisp with the cold frost of midnight; between those gloomy olive trees

I see a man, I hear him groan out his life in prayer; hearken; angels; hearken men, and wonder; it is the Savior groaning out his soul! Come and see him. Behold his brow! O heavens! Drops of blood are streaming down his face, and from his body; every pore is open, and it sweats! But not the sweat of men that toil for bread; it is the sweat of one who toils for heaven—he "sweats great drops of blood!"

That is blood-shedding, without which there is no remission. Follow that man further. They have dragged him with sacrilegious hands from the place of his prayer and his agony, and they have taken him to the hall of Pilate; they seat him in a chair and mock him; a robe of purple is put on his shoulders in mockery; and mark his brow. They have put about it a crown of thorns, and crimson drops of gore (blood) are rushing down his cheeks! Ye angels! The drops of blood are running down his cheeks! But turn aside that purple robe for a moment. His back is bleeding. Tell me, demons did this. They lift up the thongs, still dripping drops of gore; they scourge and tear his flesh, and make a river of blood to run down his shoulders! That is the shedding of blood without which there is no remission. Not yet have I done: they hurry him through the streets; they fling him on the ground; they nail his hands and his feet to the transverse wood. They hoist it in the air, they dash it into its socket, it is fixed, and there he hangs, the Christ of God. Blood from his head, blood from his hands, blood from his feet! In agony unknown he bleeds away his life; in terrible throes he exhausts his soul. "Eloi, Eloi, lama sabacthani." This is the shedding of blood, sinners and saints; this is the awful shedding of blood, the terrible pouring out of blood without which for you, and for the whole human race, there is no remission... Why is it that this story doth not make men weep?...Oh! If our hearts were but soft as iron, we must weep if they were, but tender as the marble of the mountains, we should shed great drops of grief; but they are harder than the nether millstone; we forget the griefs of him that died that ignominious death. We pity not his sorrows, nor do we account the interest we have in him as though he suffered and accomplished all for us. Nevertheless here stands the principle—"Without the shedding of blood there is no remission.[20]

How soon we forget all that Christ did for us there on that old rugged cross. He died in your place and mine. It was my sin and yours that nailed Him to the cross. He who knew no sin was made to be sin for us that we might become the righteousness of God in Him. Yes, the perfect, blameless, spotless, Son of God shed His blood for you and me.

If we fail to grasp how exceedingly sinful our sin really is, and how God's justice demands the death penalty for sin, then we will never appreciate all that Christ did for us. If someone walked up to me and told me they had paid a large sum for a debt I owed, I would laugh at them if I wasn't aware that I had a debt. It is only after being informed for years that my debt had been growing that I can appreciate the one who paid it for me.

We often sing "Amazing Grace" without the realization of what that grace cost. Perhaps it would be even more poignant and meaningful if we sang it this way:

> *Amazing grace how sweet the sound*
> *That saved a wretch like me*
> *It cost the Son of God His life*
> *To give that grace to me.*

Thank God for His grace, but grace alone was not sufficient to provide us with forgiveness. One of the essential qualities of God's character is His graciousness. When Moses pleaded with God to be shown His glory, we are told, "Then the Lord passed by in front of him and proclaimed. 'The Lord, the Lord God, compassionate and gracious, slow to anger, and abounding in lovingkindness and truth, who keeps lovingkindness for thousands, who forgives iniquity, transgression and sin...'" (Exod. 34:6-7). Yet in order for God's graciousness to be released, His justice has to be satisfied. It was only through the shed blood of Christ that this was possible.

This has always presented man with a problem. How do you extend mercy while at the same time showing yourself to be just? It was this very dilemma that caused King Darius a sleepless night. Darius, you recall, had been tricked into issuing a decree that anyone found praying to any god besides the king should be thrown into the lion's den. After the king signed the decree, it immediately became law. The penalty, if broken, was death by the mouths of lions. When the king was informed that his friend Daniel had violated his law, he had no option but to throw Daniel into the lion's den. Failure to have done so would have undermined the whole judicial system of Babylon and made a mockery of the king's rule of law.

Let's pick up the story from Daniel 6:14: "Then, as soon as the king heard this statement, he was deeply distressed and set his mind on delivering Daniel; and even until sunset he kept exerting himself to rescue him." It is clear from this verse that the king desired to be gracious and merciful to his friend, Daniel. He spends the night racking his mind as to how to be both just and the justifier. If he shows favor to Daniel, then his law becomes meaningless. If he insists on upholding his law, then Daniel is faced with certain death.

Just as Darius was unable to provide both justice and mercy, God in His infinite wisdom was able to fully satisfy His justice and at the same time provide mercy and grace through the death of His son. As the hymn writer penned it so beautifully:

> In my place condemned He stood
> Sealed my pardon with his blood
> Hallelujah, what a Savior.[21]

It was only because of the shed blood of the Lamb that you and I could know freedom from God's wrath and thereby receive His grace. It will take us all of eternity to fully comprehend all that Jesus endured for us on the cross. The very least we can do to show our love and gratitude is to offer Him our lives as a living sacrifice in return for all He has done for us.

Before closing this chapter, I need to mention something about genuine repentance. Without repentance, God's grace toward us, while available, is inoperable. This can best be illustrated by the following story from Dr. G. Campbell Morgan:

> Dr. Pierson once gave me a great illustration on this subject. He told me how in one of the Southern States a man lay condemned to die for having murdered another man; and a brother of the condemned murderer, who himself was a pure, strong man and had laid the State under obligation to him, went and pleaded the cause of his condemned brother with the authorities. Though the case was one of clear murder, though there was no question about it, for the sake of the brother who had saved lives, they consented to pardon the brother who had taken life. Then he went with the pardon of his condemned brother in his possession. He did not tell him immediately, but presently in talking to him, he said to him. "If you had your pardon, supposing you had it now, and you were to go out free, what would you do?" And with a gleam of malice and hatred in his eye, the murderer said, "I would find the principal witness and I would kill him, and I would kill the judge." And that brother said nothing of the pardon. Leaving the cell he tore it

to pieces and destroyed it, and you know that he did what was right.

Pardon for a man who is insisting in sin is impossible. It would continue the disorder, and make it infinitely worse. God will pardon you even though you cannot undo your past, pardon you without any merit on your part, but if in your heart you still cling to sin, He cannot, dare not, pardon you. And that is why the condition of receiving remission is repentance toward God. And repentance does not mean that a man quits sinning. It means that he is willing to quit if but the power be given him to do it. Are you willing to cease, if only the past may be dealt with, and power be given to you by which you shall sin no more? That is repentance.[22]

Even though God is loving and gracious, He cannot simply dismiss our sin. To do so would prove He did not love us. I carry in my Bible a small yellow sticky note on which I photocopied the following:

All this talk about God being such a God of love that He passes lightly over sin is the misunderstanding of what sin is. Love is the sworn foe of sin forever, and the instant God begins to excuse sin, as we are too often rashly doing, He proves He does not love man. Narrow that down to your own personality, or rather let me speak of mine. If God excuses sin in me, and lets me go on, just saying, "Well he is frail and infirm. It does not matter," God Himself, by such action, ensures my sin. It is because He is a consuming fire to sin, and never signs a truce with it within the sphere of His own kingdom, or in the world anywhere, that He is a God of love....[23]

[18] Mark Meynell. *Cross-Examined.* (Downers Grove, IL: InterVarsity Press, 2001), 118. Used by permission of InterVarsity Press.

[19] Ibid.

[20] Charles H. Spurgeon. *Metropolitan Tabernacle Pulpit*, Vol. 3. (Pasadena, TX: Pilgrim Publications, 1971), 90.

[21] Philip P. Bliss, *Hymns of Glorious Praise.* "Hallelujah! What a Savior!" (Springfield, MO: Gospel Publishing House, 1969), 103.

[22] G. Campbell Morgan. *The Westminster Pulpit.* Vol. 6. (New York: Flemming H. Revel Company, 1954), 72.

23 W. R. Moody, *Record of Christian Work.* (New York, Flemming H. Revel Company, 1808), 131.

In Whom We Have Redemption Through His Blood

CHAPTER FOURTEEN

The Passover

Then Moses called for all the elders of Israel,
and said to them, "Go take for yourselves lambs
according to your families, and slay the Passover lamb.

EXODUS 12:21

The Old Testament abounds with types and shadows, illustrating God's great and glorious plan of redemption for man. However, nowhere is that better portrayed for us than as we see it revealed through the Feast of the Passover. The Passover can be summed up in the words of the first song that Moses and Israel sang upon their deliverance from Egypt. Exodus 15:13–16 says:

> *In Thy loving kindness Thou hast led the people*
> *whom Thou hast redeemed;*
> *In Thy strength Thou hast guided them*
> *To Thy holy habitation…*
> *Terror and dread fall upon them*
> *By the greatness of Thine arm*
> *They are motionless as stone;*
> *Until Thy people pass over, O Lord*
> *Until Thy people pass over*
> *Whom Thou hast purchased.*

Israel was purchased for God by the blood of a lamb— clearly a foreshadowing of God's intended purpose He was to accomplish through the death of His Son almost two thousand years later.

Before we take an in-depth look at the Passover, we want to first look at the circumstances Israel was facing prior to their release from bondage.

Joseph was sent by God to prepare the way for the remainder of his family to join him in Egypt. Famine had gripped the region where he had been raised, causing his brothers to make their way to Egypt in search of food. By this time Joseph had risen up through the ranks and now found himself presiding over the day-to-day affairs of Egypt. After making himself known to his brothers, he eventually convinced them to migrate to Egypt, along with their father, Jacob. Israel as a nation began to flourish during this time. The seventy people that initially migrated grew grown into tens of thousands. Following the death of Pharaoh, another king arose who felt threatened by the rapid expansion of Israel. His solution was to place them under taskmasters and force them into slavery. These years of bondage are referred to in the Bible as the "iron furnace of affliction." As the pressure mounted, Israel cried out, and God responded by sending them Moses. Moses had previously tried through his own efforts to deliver his brethren but had failed.

When Moses arrives back in Egypt to confront Pharaoh, he is met with stiff resistance. Pharaoh refused to meet the demands of Moses. Israel had by this time become useful to Pharaoh as slaves. He was able to use them to further his purposes. Israel's entire existence consisted in building storage cities for Pharaoh. Day after day they labored under their taskmaster's whip, longing for freedom yet unable to do anything about it. We too are in bondage to sin. According to Paul's epistle to the Romans, "To whom you yield yourselves servants to obey, his servants you are…" We are also told that he that commits sin is a slave to sin (Rom. 6:16–17).

Returning to our story of Israel, Pharaoh tries his best to keep the children of Israel in the land. Notice if you will Pharaoh's response to Moses's demands. Keep in mind that most of these responses were punctuated by some type of plague.

1. "Go sacrifice to your God within the land" (Exod. 8:25).

2. "I will let you go…only you shall not go very far" (Exod. 8:28).

3. "Go now, the men among you, and serve the Lord" (Exod. 10:11).

4. "Go, serve the Lord; only let your flocks and your herds be detained. Even your little ones may go with you" (Exod. 10:24).

5. "Rise up, get out from among my people, both you and the sons of Israel; and go, worship the Lord, as you have said…" (Exod. 12:31).

God's plan of deliverance was to totally free His people from slavery. Pharaoh first suggests that they stay in the land and worship their God. Our enemy too would try to convince us to remain in the world and simply add God to our worldly pursuits. Pharaoh then suggests that they go but not far. The enemy has convinced many believers to stay as close as they can to the world. Pharaoh then suggests that they go but leave behind their wives and children. The devil knows that whatever we leave behind us, as long as we love that thing, we will be drawn back to it. You can see the parallel here between Pharaoh's diabolic reasoning and the way the devil seeks to maintain his control over us.

No man can serve two masters. It was only through the power of the blood that Israel could be free to serve God the way God intended.

We now turn our attention to the Passover, the first of seven feasts that God ordained for Israel. We will see the amazing parallel between this feast and its fulfillment in Christ in the New Testament. "Christ our Passover has been sacrificed for us" (1 Cor. 5:7).

Old Testament: Shadow

Institution: Exodus 12:2 "This month shall be the beginning of months for you; it is to be the first month of the year to you." The Passover commenced a new season in the life of Israel. This was to mark a new beginning; time was to forever change for them.

New Testament: The death of Christ also divided time. Regardless of whether you live in a Moslem, Communist, Buddhist, or Western country, we all recognize that this is now Anno Domini, the Year of Our Lord. Yes, Christ divided time. This is especially true for every Christian. "Therefore if any man is in Christ he is a new creature; the old things passed away; behold new things have come" (2 Cor. 5:17).

Jesus told Nicodemus, "Unless one is born again..." (John 3:3). Our new birth in Christ marks a new beginning in our life.

Reception: Every Israelite was told that they had to "each take a lamb for themselves..." (Exod. 12:3). Every household was required to take a lamb for their household. It was not sufficient just for your neighbor to do it. You had to do it personally for yourself.

New Testament: "As many as received Him, to them He gave the right to become the children of God" (John 1:12). Each person must receive Christ personally as their "lamb." Jesus is the Lamb. "Behold the Lamb of God that takes away the sin of the world" (John 1:29).

Inspection: "Your lamb shall be an unblemished male a year old." Every lamb had to be inspected prior to being killed. Only a perfect lamb could be accepted.

New Testament: "Knowing that you were not redeemed with perishable things like silver and gold...but with the precious blood, as of a lamb unblemished and spotless, the blood of Christ" (1 Peter 1:18–19). Jesus was accused by the Jews of all types of blasphemous things, and yet after Jesus was "inspected," Pilate stated, "Having examined Him I find no fault in Him" (Luke 23:14).

Execution/Crucifixion: Having chosen an unblemished lamb, they were to keep it for fourteen days. Anyone who has kept a lamb knows that you can quickly become attached to it. It would soon become part of the family, so to speak. Yet on the fourteenth day at twilight, it was to be killed. "Then the whole congregation of Israel is to kill it at twilight" (Exod. 12:6).

New Testament: "Let Him be crucified...at the sixth hour darkness fell" (Matt. 27:22, 45).

Application/Appropriation: Israel was then told by the Lord to apply the blood to the door posts of their houses. "Moreover they shall take some of the blood and put it on the two doorposts and on the lentil of the houses in which they eat it" (Exod. 12:7). The shed blood alone was not sufficient to save them. The blood had to be applied personally.

New Testament: "Without the shedding of blood there is no forgiveness of sin" (Heb. 9:22). "For by grace are you saved through faith…" (Eph. 2:8–9). While there is no forgiveness apart from the blood of Christ, neither is there forgiveness unless the sinner appropriates that blood by faith.

Confession: "Put it on the two doorposts…" The blood was not placed inside their houses but on the outside—on the doorposts. It was visible to the world and a testimony that they were placing their faith in God to save them.

New Testament: "If you confess with your mouth Jesus as Lord and believe in your heart…you will be saved" (Rom. 10:9). Too many believers fail to publicly acknowledge that they have accepted Christ as Lord and Savior.

Impartation: Following the application of the blood to their doorposts, they were to roast the lamb and then eat it. "And they shall eat the flesh the same night, roasted with fire…" (Exod. 12:8). They were to derive their strength from partaking of the lamb.

New Testament: Jesus told His disciples, "Unless you eat the flesh of the Son of man and drink His blood, you have no life in yourselves" (John 6:53). "But if the Spirit of Him who raised Jesus from the dead dwells in you. He who raised Jesus from the dead will also give life to your mortal bodies through His Spirit who indwells you" (Rom. 8:11).

Separation: Immediately following the meal, they were to set out on their journey and leave Egypt behind them. "Now you shall eat it in this manner: with your loins girded, your sandals on your feet, and your staff in your hand; and you shall eat it in haste" (Exod. 12:11).

New Testament: "He has delivered us out of the kingdom of darkness..." (Col. 1:13). The Christian life is to be a life of separation from the world. "Love not the world, neither the things that are in the world..." (1 John 2:15). We are exhorted, "Come out from among them and be separate..." (2 Cor. 6:17).

Exaltation/Dominion: God promised the Israelites that He would not only destroy all the firstborn in Egypt but that He would also show His supremacy over all their gods. "And against all the gods of Egypt I will execute judgments—I am the Lord" (Exod. 12:12).

New Testament: Paul in his letter to the Colossians tells us, "He has disarmed rulers and authorities...triumphed over them" (Col. 2:15). When Jesus died and rose again, He displayed His supremacy over all other power and authority. He has been given a name that is above every name. He is Lord.

Liberation: "When I see the blood I will pass over you and no plague shall destroy you" (Exod. 12:13). "Remember this day in which you went out from Egypt, from the house of slavery..." (Exod. 13:3). The Passover liberated the children of Israel from the house of bondage and from Pharaoh's dominion over them.

New Testament: "Who gave Himself for our sins, that He might deliver us out of this present evil age" (Gal. 1:4). "It was for freedom that Christ set us free; therefore keep standing firm."

Celebration: The entire Passover was to be celebrated as a feast to the Lord. "Now this day will be a memorial to you, and you shall celebrate it as a feast to the Lord; throughout your generations…"

New Testament: "For Christ our Passover also has been sacrificed. Let us therefore celebrate the feast…" (1 Cor. 5:7–8). "Every time we partake of the communion we celebrate Christ's death. Do this in remembrance of me" (1 Cor. 11:24).

Sanctification: "Seven days you shall eat unleavened bread, but on the first day you shall remove leaven from your houses…" (Exod. 12:15).

New Testament: "Clean out the old leaven that you may be a new lump…" (1 Cor. 5:7). "Therefore if any man cleanses himself from these things, he will be a vessel for honor, sanctified, useful to the Master, prepared for every good work" (2 Tim. 2:21).

Unification: "It is to be eaten in a single house; you are not to bring forth any of the flesh outside the house, nor are you to break any bone of it" (Exod. 12:46).

NEW TESTAMENT: "The Jews therefore, because it was the day of preparation, so that the bodies should not remain on the cross on the Sabbath, asked Pilate that their legs might be broken…but coming to Jesus, when they saw that He was already dead, they did not break the legs...for these things came to pass, that the Scripture might be fulfilled, 'Not a bone of Him shall be broken'" (John 19:31–36).

Progression/Submission: Israel was not to remain stagnant but to set out from Egypt pursuing God's purpose for them. "And the Lord was going before them in a pillar of cloud by day to lead them on the way..." (Exod. 13:21).

New Testament: "For all who are being led by the Spirit of God, these are the sons of God" (Rom. 8:14).

Redemption: "Until Thy people pass over, O Lord, until Thy people pass over whom Thou has purchased" (Exod. 15:6).

New Testament: "For Thou wast slain and didst purchase for God with Thy blood, men..." (Rev. 5:9).

Immersion: "And the sons of Israel went through the midst of the sea on the dry land, and the waters were like a wall to them on their right hand and on their left" (Exod. 14:22). "Pharaoh's chariots and his army He has cast into the sea and the choicest of his officers are drowned in the Red Sea" (Exod. 15:4).

New Testament: "Therefore we have been buried with Him through baptism unto death, in order that as Christ was raised from the dead through the glory of the Father, so we too might walk in newness of life...that we should no longer be slaves to sin" (Rom. 6:4–6).

I think you can see from these verses how the Old Testament Passover was fulfilled in every detail through the atoning work of the Lord Jesus Christ. I could list numerous other New Testament Scriptures that give further support to all we have covered in this brief study.

In the following chapter, I write about the Feast of Unleavened Bread.

CHAPTER FIFTEEN

Eternal Security and the Feast of Unleavened Bread

Seven days you shall eat unleavened bread, but on the first day you shall remove leaven from your houses; for whoever eats anything leavened from the first day until the seventh day, that person shall be cut off from Israel.

EXODUS 12:15

The debate over eternal security has been going on for centuries and will no doubt continue long after my life has passed. For some, this doctrine holds the same importance to them as the doctrine of the Trinity or the Virgin Birth. To question it is tantamount to heresy. Churches have argued it over it, denominations have divided over it, friends have become foes over it, and families have fought over it.

Why all this fervor, fussing, and fuming over whether you can lose your salvation or not? I remember when the argument arose over whether a Christian could have a demon. One Smart Alec replied, "Yes, if he wants one!" I know I'm not about to settle this issue in just a few lines or volumes, for that matter. I never really gave a great deal of thought to this issue, as I was raised with the belief that you can lose your salvation. For me it was a nonissue. I was right, and the opposing side was simply wrong! I have, since that time, tried to read books presenting the other viewpoint so I could become familiar with what they believe.

Like most hotly debated topics, there are always two sides to an argument. When faced with the evidence to support one viewpoint, it appears to be a clear-cut case. However, when the other viewpoint is given, along with some scriptural support, you once again find yourself not knowing what to believe.

Several years ago as I was studying the Feasts of the Lord, I was meditating on the Feast of Unleavened Bread. Keep in mind that this feast began immediately after the Passover ended. For this reason, they are often linked together. We could say that the Passover gave Israel protection, provision, and promise, while the Feast of Unleavened Bread spoke of purity or penalty, among other things. Leaven throughout the Bible is almost, without exception, a type of sin. Leaven, while small in quantity, soon became a catalyst for change. Leaven would cause the dough it was placed in to raise until all was affected by it. Leaven works best in a lukewarm environment. Although it cannot be heard or seen, its effect can be seen.

One can readily see how this typifies the way sin operates unless dealt with. It may appear to be small and insignificant at the beginning, but if allowed to have its way, it soon affects everything. God often used pictorial language to teach his people. Leaven was a part of their everyday life. In those days, they didn't drive to the supermarket to purchase their bread but rather baked it in their own homes. Before placing all the dough in the oven, a small portion was kept aside to be used the next day.

God was revealing to the children of Israel that although they were redeemed by the blood, and through no work of their own, they were now responsible to walk in obedience to His Word. It was now their responsibility to keep themselves pure. They were responsible for removing any trace of leaven from their homes. The Feast of Unleavened Bread lasted seven days. Seven in the Bible is always the number of completion. God was showing Israel that this was to be a lifestyle. Even though the feast only lasted for seven days, it symbolized God's intention for them to live a sanctified life of separation from sin. If any Israelite failed to remove the leaven from their home they were to be cut off from Israel (Exod. 11:15). This may seem like too severe a penalty, but when we consider what leaven represented, we also see God's hatred toward sin. I believe it was Robert Govett who made the statement that there were two ways an Israelite could be cut off. One was the failure to apply the blood to the doorpost of his house. The other, he said, was if after applying the blood, he failed to remove the leaven from his house.

I believe God was sending a strong but clear message to every believer that He intends His children to live a life of purity and obedience to His Word. "Let everyone that nameth the name of the Lord, depart from iniquity" (2 Tim. 2:19). Sadly the Church seems to have distorted God's grace to mean it doesn't matter how you live once you are "under the blood."

Now one could argue that I'm basing my belief in the pictorial language of the Old Testament and not the New Testament. Well let's look at how this was applied to a New-Testament believer. In 1 Corinthians 5, the apostle Paul writes to the Corinthian believers about a report that has reached him. It concerned one of their members who was involved in gross sexual immorality. Paul describes the immorality as something unheard of even among the Gentiles. This member of the Corinthian church was sexually involved with his father's wife. Paul reproves them first of all for not removing this man from their midst. Instead they had become arrogant. Paul then tells them that this man is to be delivered over to Satan for the destruction of his flesh that his soul might be saved in the day of the Lord Jesus. If his soul could not be lost, then this whole act of discipline was in vain.

What is so interesting in this passage is that Paul draws from the Feast of Unleavened Bread for his actions. He reminds the Corinthians, "Do you not know that a little leaven leavens the whole lump of dough?" Paul is concerned that if left alone, this immorality will destroy the entire Church. He follows this by telling the church to "clean out the old leaven...for Christ our Passover also has been sacrificed. Therefore let us celebrate the feast, not with the old leaven, nor with the leaven of malice and wickedness, but with the unleavened bread of sincerity and truth." Paul concludes this portion with, "Remove the wicked man from among yourselves."

Here we have an excellent example of "cutting off " an individual. One could argue that this simply implies removing him from fellowship. I can grant you that, but Paul makes it clear that this discipline was in order to save his soul. Again I ask you, if his soul was "eternally secure," then how could it be lost?

The Bible is very clear that as Christians we are to live godly lives. Nowhere in God's Word are we ever given the right to live in sin. When the angel announced to Joseph that Mary was going to have a child, he said, "Joseph son of David, do not be afraid to take Mary as your wife...and she will bear a son; and you shall call His name Jesus, for it is He who will save His people from their sins" (Matt. 1:20–21). Notice the angel did not say He will save His people in their sin but from their sin. You cannot be saved from drowning and remain in the lake. You cannot be saved from the fire and remain in the flames. You cannot be saved from bankruptcy and still be bankrupt. Grace was never intended to provide an excuse for sin. Paul tells the believers in Rome, "Sin shall not be master over you, for you are not under law, but under grace." Here we are told the power of grace is greater than the power of sin.

Finally, in seeking to conclude this matter, I would like to share some correspondence from the famous Dr. Campbell G. Morgan taken from the book *This Was His Faith*. These are a collection of letters that he wrote over the course of his ministry. He writes:

> The question you raise is a very large one…It has been under discussion for centuries, and is a theological problem which has divided the Christian Church into two separate camps known as the Calvinists and the Arminian. The Calvinists teach that once a man has received the gift of life it is impossible for him to lose it. The Arminians, on the other hand, believe that the gift of life was received upon fulfillment of certain conditions on the part of man. Personally, I take the second position, and believe that it is possible for a man to fall away from grace.

> This, however, is the question that cannot be finally settled because I believe both positions are right, that is, in so far as they are based on Scripture. In so far as the question is practical it must be faced. Man's freedom of will and responsibility are clearly

and emphatically and uniformly taught in the Scriptures of truth. To state against this the fact of God, and to argue that His foreknowledge necessarily means causation, is contrary to the teaching of these selfsame Scriptures.

I know the difficulty of clearly stating these great facts, but anyone who flings back the responsibility of conduct and character upon the election of God is guilty of charging God with being the author of confusion. We must postpone to the more perfect understanding of the coming Light attempts to reconcile two views which appear to contradict each other, yet which seem to be defensible from Scripture.[24]

In another letter he writes.

I was brought up in the atmosphere of the severest Calvinism...My own study of the Word compelled me to abandon it. I realized the difficulty of attempting to reconcile the Sovereignty of God with the Free Will of man, and in many senses I suppose people would call me Calvinistic. Nevertheless I am convinced that while the thing is very improbable, it is possible to apostatize, with the inevitable consequence of being lost.[25]

In yet another letter he writes, "It is interesting to know that Arminius was engaged in writing a book in answer to one attacking Calvinism when he was driven to the conclusion that the position taken by the writer of that book was the true one."[26]

My father Leonard Ravenhill, said, "There is something wrong with the preacher's head as well as his heart, if he spends more time telling the saved they cannot be lost, than he does telling the lost that they can be saved."

It is not my intention to go into anymore detail regarding whether a person can lose his or her salvation or not. There are numerous other verses that support this viewpoint, but I feel I should leave it here.

---

[24] Jill Morgan. *This Was His Faith*. The Expository Letters of G. Campbell Morgan. (London: Pickering & Inglis Ltd., 1936), 238.

[25] Ibid., 239.

[26] Ibid, 240.

Eternal Security and the Feast of Unleavened Bread

CHAPTER SIXTEEN

Can God Lose
What He Has Saved?

Will a man rob God? Yet you are robbing Me!

But you say how have we robbed Thee?

MALACHI 3:8

When we hear about the doctrine of "eternal security," we inevitably apply it to ourselves. We argue over whether man can be lost. But what about God's rights in all of this? We need to ask ourselves the more important question, "Can God lose what he has saved?" This is a question you are unlikely to ever hear, but nevertheless, it need to be asked.

The prophet Malachi asked the question of the nation of Israel, "Will a man rob God?" The prophet then replies, "Yet you are robbing me!" Israel responds with, "How have we robbed Thee?" God responds through his prophet, "In tithes and offerings...for you are robbing me the whole nation of you!"

This passage teaches that God can be deprived or robbed of something that is rightfully His. In this case it is His tithes. While Israel no doubt thought they were getting by with it, God said "You are cursed with a curse..."

Now if this is true concerning the withholding of money, how much more does this apply to the withholding of our lives? If we are bought with a price, we are His and not our own. If we withhold from God that which is rightfully His, we are guilty of robbing Him.

John Piper in his book *The Passion of Jesus Christ* has a chapter titled "So That We Might Belong to Him." Here is what he writes:

> The ultimate question is not who you are but whose you are. Of course, many people think they are

nobody's slave. They dream of total independence. Like a jellyfish carried by the tides feels free because it isn't fastened down with the bondage of barnacles. But Jesus had a word for people who thought that way. He said, 'You will know the truth, and the truth will set you free.' But they responded, 'we...have never been in bondage to anyone. How is it that you say, 'You will become free?' So Jesus answered, 'Truly, truly, I say to you, everyone who commits sin is a slave to sin.' (John 8:32-34)

The Bible gives no reality to fallen humans who are ultimately self-determining. There is no autonomy in a fallen world. We are governed by sin or governed by God. 'You are slaves of the one whom you obey...When you were slaves of sin, you were free in regard to righteousness...But now...you have been set free from sin and have become slaves of God.' (Romans 6:16, 20, 22)

Most of the time we are free to do what we want. But we are not free to want what we ought. For that we need a new power based on a divine purchase. The power is God's. Which is why the Bible says, 'Thanks be to God, that you who were once slaves of sin have now become obedient from the heart.' (Romans 6:17) God is the one who may 'grant them repentance leading to a knowledge of the truth, and they may escape from the snare of the devil, after being captured by him to do his will.' (2 Timothy 2:25-26)

And the purchase that unleashes this power is the death of Christ. 'You are not your own, for you have been bought with a price.' (1 Corinthians 6:19-20) And what price did Christ pay for those who trust Him? 'He obtained (them) with his own blood.' (Acts 20:28)

Now we are free indeed. Not to be autonomous, but to want what is good. A whole new way of life opens to us when the death of Christ becomes the death of our old self. Relationship with the living Christ replaces rules. And the freedom of fruit bearing replaces the bondage of the law. 'You also having died to the law through the body of Christ, so that you may belong to another, to Him who was raised from the dead, in order that we may bear fruit for God.' (Romans 7:14)

Christ suffered and died that we might be set free from the law and sin and belong to Him. Here is where obedience ceases to be a burden and becomes the freedom of fruit bearing. Remember, you are not your own. Whose will you be? If Christ's, then come and belong.[27]

Why has this type of message become so rare today? Whatever happened to the teaching of death to self and alive to God? The biggest challenge facing the Church today is the rapid spread of radical Islam. This religion has stolen from the Church the message of death to self. One of the reasons why the United States and other superpowers are unable to stop the spread of this false religion is the willingness of its followers to lay down their lives for its cause. Without a doubt, it is due to this type of self-sacrifice that they have been able to make major inroads where the Church has been unable to penetrate. It was this mindset that made the Moravians so effective in their desire to take the gospel to the ends of the earth. This great praying missionary movement of the 1700s, led by Count Zinzendorf, placed the love of God and their love for the souls of men ahead of any or all love for self. Here is how David Smithers recounts their story:

> For Zinzendorf, loving fellowship with Christ was the essential manifestation of the Christian life. Throughout the Count's life 'His blessed presence' was his all consuming theme. He had chosen from an early age as his life-motto the now famous confession; 'I have one passion; it is Jesus, Jesus only.' As Zinzendorf 's passion for Jesus grew, so did his passion for the lost. He became determined to evangelize the world with a handful of saints, equipped only with a burning love for Jesus and the power of prayer. The Moravian Brotherhood readily received and perpetuated the passion of their leader. A seal was designed to express their newfound missionary zeal. The seal was composed of a lamb on a crimson ground, with the cross of resurrection and a banner of triumph with the motto; 'Our Lamb has conquered, let us follow Him.' The Moravians recognized themselves in debt to the world as the trustees of the gospel. They were taught to embrace

a lifestyle of self-denial, sacrifice and prompt obedience. They followed the call of the Lamb to go anywhere and with an emphasis upon the worst and hardest places as having the first claim. No soldiers of the cross have ever been bolder as pioneers, more patient or persistent in difficulties, more heroic in suffering, or more entirely devoted to Christ and the souls of men than the Moravian Brotherhood.

The Moravians had learned that the secret of loving the souls of men was found in loving the Savior of men. On October 8, 1732, a Dutch ship left the Copenhagen harbor bound for the Danish West Indies. On board were the two first Moravian missionaries; John Leonard Dober, a potter, and David Nitschman, a carpenter. Both were skilled speakers and ready to sell themselves into slavery to reach the slaves of the West Indies. As the ship slipped away, they lifted up a cry that would one day become the rallying call for all Moravian missionaries, "May the Lamb that was slain receive the reward of His suffering." The Moravians' passion for souls was surpassed only by their passion for the Lamb of God, Jesus Christ.

The Moravians had come to understand the truth that they were no longer their own. As Smithers states, their rallying cry became the now famous saying, "May the Lamb that was slain receive the reward of His suffering." This is taken from Isaiah's prophesy of the Lord Jesus Christ when he wrote concerning His death, 'He will see of the travail of His soul and be satisfied.' This can only refer to what John describes to us in Revelation when he saw the lamb standing as if slain and then heard that great anthem of praise, 'Worthy art Thou to take the book and to break its seals; for Thou wast slain, and didst purchase for God with Thy blood men from every tribe and tongue and people and nation...' This was the reward of His travail. This was why He paid the supreme price—His blood. It was not so much for sin as it was for saints. Yes, the sin of man had to be atoned for but it was ultimately "that He might redeem for Himself a people."[28]

Imagine you have received a quote for the cost of painting your house. The estimate is far greater than you ever envisioned. While the house may be in desperate need of paint, you are unable to pay the price. Talking to a friend one day, you explain the predicament you are in.

Without any hint on your part, he offers to do the job for you without cost. The offer seems too good to be true, but to your amazement, he begins. For several weeks he works all day from early morning to late in the evening. As the completion of the painting draws near, you decide that the least you can do is to give him a token of your deep appreciation for all he has done. You discuss the matter with your wife and decide to buy him something you know he utterly detests and has a hatred for. To do such a thing would be the greatest insult to your friend and friendship. But isn't this the very way we respond to all that Christ has done on our behalf? We give Him the one thing He hates—sin—and yet we refrain from giving Him the one thing He died to purchase—ourselves.

MAY THE LAMB THAT WAS SLAIN
RECEIVE THE REWARD OF HIS SUFFERING!

---

[27] John Piper, *The Passion of Jesus Christ*. (Wheaton, IL: Crossway, 2004), 64–65.
Used by permission of Crossway, a publishing ministry of Good News Publishers.

[28] David Smithers. Article Count Zinzendorf and the Moravians. Taken from www.watchword.org.

Can God Lose What He Has Saved?

CHAPTER SEVENTEEN

Love Slaves

But if the slave plainly says, "I love my master, my wife
and my children; I will not go out as a free man,"
then his master shall bring him to God, then he shall bring
him to the door or the doorpost. And his master shall pierce
his ear with an awl; and he shall serve him permanently.

EXODUS 21:5-6

All Americans prize their liberty. A large part of our nation's annual budget goes toward defending our freedom. The thought of losing our freedom would be unheard of. On the Fourth of July every year we gather with friends and family to celebrate our independence. The only alternative to liberty is bondage or slavery. The thought of slavery takes us back to some dark days in our nation's history when men and women were sold and traded like cattle, and oftentimes treated worse.

Just as the thought of returning to slavery is repulsive to us, so also is the thought of slavery in the spiritual realm. Here again we prize and proclaim our freedom: "Stand fast in the liberty wherein Christ has set us free and be not entangled again with the yoke of bondage." (Gal. 5:1) Christians have been liberated from sin's bondage. "My chains fell off my heart was free..." ("Amazing Grace," John Newton 1725-1807). We have even successfully eliminated the very word slave from our New Testament by using instead the word "servant." Now when we think of a servant, we understand that they have the right to come and go as they please. They have simply chosen to serve, rather like a waitress or airline attendant. The fact is that a large percentage of our nation works in the "service" sector. The idea of being called a slave does not sit well with us. A slave implies a Master or Lord, someone who we have to submit to. A slave is also someone who has lost his or her freedom and is instead under the authority of another.

No wonder we have tried to eliminate the message of lordship from our pulpits. This is not the message that results in church growth. People are far less likely to attend when presented with claims of lordship, as they would rather hear how they can achieve wealth and fame instead. Books on self-improvement far outweigh those dealing with death to self. It is this selective approach to teaching and preaching that has emasculated the Church and rendered her passionless, powerless, and purposeless.

The secret to those who overcame the enemy lay in the fact that they loved not their lives unto death. Today we love our lives so much that we are unwilling to surrender our lives in the service of the very one who redeemed us for Himself.

As the Church retreats from her calling, Islam is quickly filling the vacuum. They offer a calling and a cause bigger than living for self—a cause they are fully prepared to die for in order to see achieved. It is this willingness to die to self that has the most powerful nations on earth baffled as to how they can stop them. This is one of the underlying secrets to the rapid spread of Islam around the world and even within our own nation.

It is only when we are prepared to offer ourselves without reservation to God that we will see His Kingdom come and His will being done. The secret to this lies in whether we love God more than we love ourselves.

I love the story of Jacob, who, after fleeing from his brother Esau, finds his way to his uncle Laban's house. There he meets Laban's daughter, Rachel. Immediately he falls head over heels in love with her and seeks to take her as his wife. Laban agrees to the marriage, with one stipulation. Jacob will have to work for seven years in order to have her as his wife.

Talk about real love! Someone has said that lust can only wait seven seconds while love can wait seven years. Jacob could have easily walked away from the deal, citing that it was way too costly both in time as well as work. But no, he readily accepts and completes the required work and time allotted him. The Bible states it this way: "So Jacob served seven years for Rachel and they seemed to him but a few days because of his love for her." (Gen.29:20). Jacob gladly served because he was doing it all for Rachel. The question then is this: Are we prepared to give our lives for Christ? Are we so in love with Him that we are prepared to offer our lives in His service?

According to the Old Testament, Israel was permitted to own slaves. The slaves were either foreigners taken as captives or fellow Hebrews. In either case, they were only to serve for six years and then released in the seventh year. No doubt almost every slave would eagerly anticipate the day when he would gain his freedom again. According to the Law of Moses, God made provision whereby a slave could continue on in the service of his master. If a master showed love and kindness toward his slave, treating him more like a son than a slave, then the slave could remain. In doing so, he was taken by his master to the door of the house and there his master would pierce his ear with an awl. This testified to any and all that he was no longer serving as a common slave but as a love slave or bond slave. In a similar way, I believe the Lord is looking for those who willingly return to their heavenly Master and say, "Because of Your amazing love that rescued me from a life of sin and death, I lovingly and wholeheartedly offer You my life."

The Scripture makes it clear that God has a twofold claim on our lives. First we are His because He created us. And second, we are His because He redeemed us. Although God can exercise His prerogative over us at any time, He refuses to do so but tenderly waits for us to respond to His love.

Love must be the basis of all service. In the Song of Songs we have the story of the Bride and Bridegroom. The book commences with her longing to be kissed by her beloved. She tells him, "Your love is better than wine." In other words, she has found something that gratifies and satisfies more than anything the world has to offer her. Wine is used by the world as a coping mechanism, to drown their sorrows, fear, troubles, and pain. She has found everything she needs in the embrace and affection of her beloved. Soon after falling in love, she asks him, "Tell me where do you pasture the flock?" She realizes that she has fallen in love with a shepherd and expresses interest in his interests. We have all heard the expression a "golf widow." This is someone who falls in love but after the honeymoon is over has come to realize that her beloved is a golfer. She is faced with the choice of learning the game or sitting alone every day.

If we truly fall in love with Jesus Christ as Lord and Master, then we will also fall in love with His purposes. Our prayer will be, "Thy Kingdom come, Thy will be done." To fall in love with the Lord means we fall in love with the Great Shepherd of the sheep; therefore, we had better love the flock as He loves the flock. We fall in love with the King of kings, so we had better learn to rule and reign. We fall in love with the Great Physician, so we had better learn to bind up one another's wounds. We fall in love with the Judge of all the earth, so we had better learn to pass righteous judgment. What incredible opportunities await those who truly fall in love with Jesus Christ. There is nothing on earth that can compare to the privilege of being called to know Him and labor with Him. It is only after we surrender to His lordship that we discover why we were created.

Imagine this rather homespun illustration. A priceless Stradivarius violin has for years been lying on a shelf in some warehouse. The owner of the warehouse decides to retire and sell off his "junk" in an auction. The violin is placed on a table, along with hundreds of other items.

Each is marked with a lot number for any potential buyer to identify it by. Just prior to the auction, a young musician notices the violin and upon examining it discovers that it is a genuine "Strad." Hiding his excitement, he patiently waits for it to be auctioned off. As nobody else seemed interested in the violin, he is able to buy it for a mere fifty-five dollars. With the violin now his, he takes it to a friend who is a violin maker.

His friend can't believe his eyes when he sees the violin. After cleaning and restringing the instrument, he tunes it and then begins to play it. The tonal quality is unlike anything he has ever heard before, far surpassing anything he has ever made himself. Before handing the instrument back to his friend, he tells him if he ever wants to sell it that he could easily sell it for over a hundred thousand dollars. Now just imagine if the violin was able to talk. You might hear it say something like this: "For the past few years I had no purpose in life. I didn't really know why I was here, until one day somebody saw my value and bought me. Not only that, but they realized who created me and why. My new master deeply loves me and delights to use me for his pleasure. As I submit myself to his control I find my greatest joy and fulfillment."

The illustration may be somewhat simple but serves to make the point that apart from being "played by the master," life will never really makes sense. Isn't this what Jesus meant when He said, "He that seeks to save his life will lose it but whoever loses his life will find it"? You have nothing to lose and everything to gain by giving back to God that which He died to redeem for Himself. Why not make this simple prayer of surrender?

Jesus, I know that You are both Lord and Christ. I now give You my complete life. Take all of me, my possessions, rights, plans, desires, friends, and future. I surrender everything to You. From this moment on, I ask that You will lead me to fulfill Your plan for my life. Thank You for the honor and privilege of serving You. I will by Your grace endeavor, from this day forward, to live for Your glory and purpose alone. Amen.

APPENDIX

I BEGAN THIS BOOK by citing Jude's admonition to "contend earnestly for the faith which was once for all delivered to the saints." Two thousand years have passed since those words were written. Since that time, the gospel has morphed into an almost unrecognizable man-centered message. In order to protect ourselves, we have developed certain words that we use in our defense. One of those words is "legalism" and another is "religion." Then in order to really hedge our bets, we have added the word "spirit." This provides us with the ultimate weapon in our arsenal: the words "religious spirit" or "legalistic spirit." Since nobody wants to be accused of having any type of "spirit," we find ourselves retreating in fear of having this leveled against us.

A religious or legalistic spirit seems to be applied to any type of spiritual discipline or work. A person having a daily devotional life is said to have a religious spirit. A pastor friend of mine recently told me of a young lady in his congregation who had had a very dramatic salvation experience. She had been delivered from a background of drinking, sex, and drug abuse. She applied to go to a certain Bible school, only to discover that the school had no restriction on drinking. She was shocked to find the students not only tipsy but also prophesying over one another. She decided to bring the matter to the attention of her supervisor and was told that she had a religious spirit and needed to get over it. It is this type of nonsense that has become a plague in the modern-day Church and robbed her of her power and purity.

One of the greatest errors the Church faces today is the false premise that "grace" absolves the believer from any and all responsibility. Grace, we are told, is free, and any attempt on our part to partner with grace destroys the very essence of what grace is all about. Yes, grace is unmerited and totally undeserved, but what about our response to grace? A bird needs both wings in order to fly, just as a man needs two legs to walk. You could examine a man's leg and declare categorically that the leg is physically perfect in every way. It has all the muscles, sinews, nerves, veins, and bones a leg needs. In fact, there is nothing the leg lacks. The only problem is that there is only one leg instead of two. The fact that there is but one leg does not detract from the perfection of that leg. But having only one leg makes it impossible to walk. In the same way, we have taught only one aspect of grace.

There is a popular Asian teacher who states that God, through his grace, has provided forgiveness for all our sins: past, present, and future. While what he says is theologically true, this was not the spirit in which grace was given. This "one leg" approach lacks the necessary balance needed to properly walk. This teaching eliminates any need of repentance on our part because our sins are already forgiven. On the surface that sounds good. After all, we would not like to be accused of working for our salvation, as that would be akin to bragging about "circumcision." Others may label us as having a religious spirit. Grace is not some commodity that God has in excess and is trying to sell at a discounted price from His heavenly warehouse. Grace is a person, the Spirit of grace. Perhaps if we viewed grace as a person instead of a commodity we would be less prone to use it for our own selfish, sinful pleasures.

What I mean is that we have a tendency to sin…that grace may abound. Grace never provides us with a license to sin. Instead grace teaches and empowers us not to sin. The Bible makes it clear that we have an advocate with the Father if we sin, not when we sin.

The beloved hymn "Amazing Grace" was written by John Newton (1725–1807). Prior to his conversion to Christ, Newton was the vilest, most debased, most disgusting sinner you would ever find. Not only was he a foul-mouthed, drunkard sailor but also a slave trader. Guye Johnson in his book *Treasury of Great Hymns and their Stories* writes of Newton, "Who could measure the depth of this man's sin? His life at sea was so full of reckless abandon to sin as to be beyond estimate. But if we could not measure the depth of his sin, how much less are we able to measure the sovereign grace that removed his sin from him as far as the east is from the west."[29]

Newton understood the meaning of grace and expressed it so wonderfully in his song, "Amazing Grace."

> *Amazing grace! How sweet the sound*
> *That saved a wretch like me!*
> *I once was lost but now I'm found*
> *Was blind but now I see*

Newton first became aware of his own wretched and lost condition which led him to the understanding of how amazing was the grace that God gave him. The second verse of his hymn reveals the true nature of grace:

> *Twas grace that taught my heart to fear*
> *And grace my fears relieved*
> *How precious did that grace appear*
> *The hour I first believed!*

I have quoted extensively from the preaching of Charles Spurgeon. Allow me, if you will, to quote from him again:

> "For sin shall not have dominion over you…" Has sin dominion over you? If so, then you are not a believer. I did not say "Do you sin?" If we say we have no sin, we deceive ourselves, and the truth is not in us. But I did say, "has sin dominion over you?" If there is a single cherished sin in any one of you professors, which it is obvious you cannot conquer, and perhaps too apparent that you do not try, if you sit down quietly under the yoke of it, and cherish it as a friend rather than withstand it as a foe, then that sin has got dominion over you, and you are not in Christ. You are not a child of God.[30]

This type of preaching is a far cry from the modern preacher who avoids any mention of sin lest he drive away his financial base. Today grace has become, as one person called it, "greasy grace." This type of grace is inevitably linked with ministers who have fallen morally and are looking for some type of spiritual morphine to dull their sin, pain, and shame instead of truly repenting and calling on God for mercy.

I recently heard a pastor say that grace can be compared to a police officer who pulls you over for speeding. But rather than give you a ticket, he hands you a check for one thousand dollars. If that were the case, you would never eliminate speeding but rather encourage it, since it obviously pays to speed.

Every year I travel to Singapore to speak in a Bible school there. Singapore has one of the strictest bans on the importation of illicit drugs. The death penalty! Suppose I'm caught trying to bring some drugs into the country. After having a fair trial, I'm found guilty and sentenced to die in seven days. Over the course of that week, I begin to realize the severity of my crime as well as the severity of my punishment. I'll never see my family and friends again. I'll never experience marriage and family life. I'll never be able to finish my education or travel. I'll never be able to celebrate Christmas, Thanksgiving, or a birthday ever again. As desperation sets in, I begin to plead with my guards for mercy, telling them that I am truly sorry for breaking the law of the land. Despite my cries for help, my pleas go unanswered. I'm guilty and must pay the price for my sin. Finally after all my begging and pleading has fallen on deaf ears, I'm informed I have a visitor who wants to see me. I share with him how over the course of the past week I have begun to see myself as guilty and totally deserving of my punishment and that given another chance, I would never do something so foolish again. My friend listens to me and then tells me that he will take my punishment and die in my place. In this way, he says, the law will be upheld, but I will be justified. That is *grace*.

I have always been a fan of the late William Barclay, especially his books dealing with Greek words and their background. In his book *The Mind of St. Paul*, he has a chapter titled "The Essential Grace." Toward the close of the chapter he writes:

> There remains one side of the question still to be considered, and it can only be called the obligation of grace. Twice Paul uses a suggestive phrase, once of himself and once of his converts. In 1 Corinthians 15:10 he says that the grace of God was not bestowed upon him in vain. In 2 Corinthians 6:1 he beseeches his converts not to receive the grace of God in vain. In the latter case, the phrase is eiskenon. Literally meaning, emptiness.[31]

Here is the other side of the question. It is here that the balance is preserved and that works come in. We can say that the works have nothing to do with salvation, but we dare not say that works have nothing to do with the Christian life. Paul was far too good a Jew ever to say that, for Judaism was supremely an ethical religion. Christianity was a religion that issued in a certain way of life. Was it not first titled *the Way*?

A man is saved by grace. What is the result of that? The result is that it lays upon a man the tremendous obligation to spend his life showing that grace was not expended on him in vain. Grace has reached out to him by the love God. He must therefore be filled with the unutterable longing and the burning desire to show himself by the help of that grace, worthy of that grace. This is out of the sphere of law altogether. This is not legal obligation. It is not a case of doing good and being good, but because a man cannot bear to disappoint the love that has loved him so.

Here is what is at the back of Romans 6. At the back of that chapter, there is an argument. The misguided ones say to Paul: "You believe that God's grace is the biggest thing in the world?" "Yes" answered Paul. "You believe that God's grace is wide enough to forgive any sin?" "Yes."

Then the misguided one goes on to argue, "If that be so, let us go on sinning to our heart's content. God will forgive. The more we sin, the more chances this wonderful grace of God will receive and abound. Let us continue to sin that grace may get more chances to abound."

The whole essence of that argument is that it is a legal argument. Basically it says that we can go on sinning because sin will not be punished, and grace will find a way of escape. But Paul's whole position is the lover's position. He cannot make the grace that loved him so of no effect; he must spend all his life in one great endeavor to show how much he loves the God who loved him so much.

I would add that it is this response to God's grace that underscores what this book is all about. While God has a creative and redemptive right to our life, He will not force that upon us. We must respond to His love by freely and willingly yielding ourselves to Him, acknowledging Him not only as our Savior but also as our Lord and Master. Remember:

You are not your own.
You were bought with a price!

[30] Charles H. Spurgeon. *Metropolitan Tabernacle Pulpit.* Vol. 15 Message: "The Upper Hand." (Pasadena, TX: Pilgrim Publications, Inc, 1971), 638.

[31] William Barclay, *The Mind of St. Paul. The Essential Grace.* (London: Collins, 1958), 169.

OTHER BOOKS BY DAVID RAVENHILL

For God's Sake Grow Up
They Drank From The River And Died In The Wilderness
The Jesus Letters
Surviving The Anointing
Welcome Home

LEONARD RAVENHILL BOOKS

Why Revival Tarries (Also available in Spanish)
Revival Praying
Revival God's Way
A Treasury Of Prayer
Sodom Had No Bible
Tried And Transfigured
America Is Too Young To Die
Meat For Men

All titles are available through your local Christian
bookstore or through Amazon.com

Some Leonard Ravenhill titles may be temporarily out of print.

DAVID RAVENHILL

SPEAKING ENGAGEMENTS
AND BULK BOOK ORDERS

The author, David Ravenhill, is available
to speak at churches and conferences.

Blood Bought can be purchased
in large discounted quantities.

CONTACT:
479.373.6461 or
david.ravenhill@gmail.com

CPSIA information can be obtained at www.ICGtesting.com
Printed in the USA
LVOW01s0559170614

390371LV00002B/33/P